SOMETHING
LIKE
THE GODS

A CULTURAL HISTORY OF THE ATHLETE FROM ACHILLES TO LeBRON

STEPHEN AMIDON

RODALE.

Notice

Mention of specific companies, organizations, or authorities in this book does not imply endorsement by the author or publisher, nor does mention of specific companies, organizations, or authorities imply that they endorse this book, its author, or the publisher.

Internet addresses and telephone numbers given in this book were accurate at the time it went to press.

Rodale books may be purchased for business or promotional use or for special sales. For information, please write to: Special Markets Department, Rodale Inc., 733 Third Avenue, New York, NY 10017.

Printed in the United States of America

Rodale Inc. makes every effort to use acid-free ⊗, recycled paper ♻.

Book design by Amy King

Library of Congress Cataloging-in-Publication Data

Amidon, Stephen.
  Something like the gods : a cultural history of the athlete from Achilles to LeBron / Stephen Amidon.
      p.   cm.
  Includes index.
  ISBN 978–1–60961–123–1 hardcover
  1. Sports—Social aspects—History.   2. Athletes—History.   I. Title.
GV706.5A46   2012
306.4'83—dc23   2012002365

Distributed to the trade by Macmillan

2   4   6   8   10   9   7   5   3   1 hardcover

We inspire and enable people to improve their lives and the world around them.

www.rodalebooks.com

For Alexander

The race of men is one thing, that of the gods is another.

There is a total difference in power so that we are nothing—

while the bronze heaven remains the gods' secure seat forever.

But nevertheless—we can become something like the gods,

through excellence—excellence of mind or of body;

even if we don't know from day to day—or night to night—

what finish line fate has marked for our run.

—PINDAR

CONTENTS

THE FACADE

It was 1969 and I was making my first visit to Yankee Stadium. I was 10 years old. Following the Yankees had become an obsession for me, despite the fact that it was one of those rare times in their history when they had no chance of making the World Series. I listened to as many of their games as possible on my transistor radio, read box scores as if they contained coded messages, wrote letters to the Bronx asking for autographed photos of my favorite players. I accumulated baseball cards even after my allowance ran out, occasionally taking advantage of the perfect fit of the Topps packet into the back pocket of my blue jeans, a convergence that turned an entire generation of American boys into potential petty larcenists. I would then recklessly trade away any card bearing the image of a non-Yankee, never doubting that the names Tresh, Kenney, and Bahnsen would one day enter the pantheon of immortals. I read book after book about the team and its legends. If you asked me—and people were already learning not to—I could tell you just about anything you wanted to know about the most famous sports franchise in American history.

It was Bat Day. In a practice symbolic of the era's prosperity, kids passing through the turnstiles were given a free Louisville Slugger. Not some cheap facsimile, but a real wood bat you could actually use back home in your pickup games. The stadium was already half full when we arrived. As we ascended to our seats in the upper deck, I could hear a crackling sound cutting through the oceanic stadium noise. Thousands of bats tapping against concrete and metal. After a climb that seemed to take us higher than the top of the Empire State Building, we entered the stadium itself. Upper tier, first base side, just a few rows back from the edge. Anyone who steps into a great stadium for the first time will know what I felt. The vertigo that comes not just from being on a steep terrace so high above the ground, but also from the sense that this is sacred space, that the air here is different from that out in the parking lot or back home. Later I'd enter Notre Dame de Paris and Carnegie Hall. I'd stand at the lip of the Grand Canyon and fly over a smoldering volcano in Iceland. They did not even come close.

Once we'd settled into our seats, I set about my private mission: to locate the spot I'd been desperate to see ever since I'd learned we would be coming to the stadium. Not the dugout or the pitcher's mound. Not the three famous monuments in fair play deep in center field, an array that DiMaggio supposedly once ran behind to catch a towering fly. (Every 10-year-old in the stadium could tell you that two of the monuments commemorated Gehrig and Ruth; how many knew, as I did, that the third honored Miller Huggins?) No, the point I wanted to see was on the ornate "facade," as it was called, that hung above the upper deck of the right field stands. I'd first become aware of this particular spot in a picture book I'd found in the local library. *Great Moments in Baseball History*, I think it was called. The photo in question was a panorama of the stadium, taken from the third base line. In it, players and fans were too small to be distinguishable. What you could not miss, however, were the two bold lines that had been drawn on the photo's surface. The first angled from home plate up to my magical spot at the top of the stadium. The second line dropped back down from that point to the outfield. Two sides of a right triangle of epic proportions.

According to my book, these lines traced the trajectory of the hardest hit baseball in human history. It had happened on May 22, 1963, in the 11th inning of a game against the Kansas City A's. The batter, of course, was Mickey Mantle. Although the painted photo had been impressive enough, it was not until I sat in my rickety seat that I understood the majesty of Mantle's shot. Once I had conferred with my brother to be sure I had picked out the proper point of impact, I tracked back to home plate. And then I looked back at the facade. And then back at home plate. This went on for a while, my eyes tracing and retracing the photograph's long ascending line. As those gift bats continued to ring out their fractured symphony around me and the sluggish stadium organ began to play, I entered a sort of trance. I had never experienced this sort of awe. My young brain could not process it. By all accounts, the ball was *rising* when it hit the facade. Everyone present on that mythical day, even seasoned players, swore that the sound Mantle's bat made when he got hold of the ball did not sound like anything they had ever heard. Yogi Berra, with his catcher's reflexes, was the first to leap from the dugout, shouting "That's it!" as he tracked the shot. As if this was the moment everyone had been waiting for since the day the stadium opened forty years earlier.

I could not understand how it was possible to hit a ball like that. I had arms, I'd swung a bat. I had even made pretty good contact a few times. But this bore no relation to anything I could have ever done. What I was looking at was simply beyond the realm of human ability. I also became aware of something else I hadn't expected to feel. The tragedy of that hit. If it hadn't been for that unnecessary bit of architecture (I have never had much taste for fancy facades since), the ball would have been the first to leave the stadium in fair territory. Ruth, Gehrig, DiMaggio—no one had ever hit a shot like that. Some people estimate it could have traveled over 600 feet before landing.

He was gone by the time I went to the stadium, of course. He had announced his sad retirement earlier that spring. It was years before I'd learn that he was not exactly the golden boy of my books. That he'd had an elaborate facade of his own. I would read all about the drinking, the hangovers, the mistresses, the contempt he could display for fans like me. The fact that he was a bad dad and a worse husband. Later, I'd watch his sad demise from liver cancer, and then listen to the outraged speculation that he'd jumped the donor waiting list for a transplant that had scant chance of saving him. I'd come to see that damned piece of architecture as symbolic of his injury-riddled career. Just a little bit higher, a little more lift, and he would have easily been the greatest ever. I'd watch Mark McGwire and Sammy Sosa perform their juiced-up tango; I'd try *not* to watch as Barry Bonds hit balls into San Francisco Bay with a glum arrogance that could not hide his guilt. But no subsequent knowledge would diminish the awe I felt that day. The sense that something had happened in this place that was not quite of this life, and that simply by sitting in that folding blue seat six years afterward, my Keds sticking to the beer-sodden concrete beneath me, I was taking part in it.

The athlete has always been able to transport us out of our

daily lives. He was once even considered to be a shaman. Long before stadiums and arenas, before leagues and tournaments and championships, before the NBA and the NFL, Wimbledon and the World Cup, the athlete's games were rituals. His sole intent was to please the gods. Through his exertions, he believed he could conjure rain, cure illness, and bring fertility to crops and animals. The athlete's rituals could be found in most ancient cultures. Mayans and Aztecs played an elaborate ball game that would end with players being sacrificed to their divine spectators (though it remains unclear whether those slaughtered were the game's winners or losers). In ancient Crete, young Minoan men would grab bulls by the horns, causing the furious beasts to fling them into the air, whereupon they would perform elaborate flips and twists that were believed to increase the fertility of both human and animal. And in Greece, pilgrims would gather at a shrine to Zeus in a remote spot called Olympia, where worship of their muscular god involved a series of running, wrestling, and throwing contests that would ultimately evolve into the most famous athletic festival of all.

The athlete is no longer a religious figure. Some competitors may thank Jesus or praise Allah after a big win, but their games are now strictly secular. Nonetheless, they are still expected to cast a spell. Nearly everyone who follows athletes will have felt the power those present for Mantle's home run experienced, those few seconds when a competitor stops time. Ali coming off the ropes to stun Foreman in Kinshasa. Dwight Clark pulling down Joe Montana's pass at the back of the end zone to win the 1982 NFC Championship game. Michael Jordan's game-winning jumper in the 1998 NBA finals. Brandi Chastain tearing off her jersey after her winning penalty kick in the 1999 Women's World Cup. Carlton Fisk's home run against the Reds, David Beckham's stoppage time free kick against Greece, Doug Flutie's Hail Mary pass against the University of Miami, Bob Beamon's endless leap through the thin Mexico City air, Nadia's twenty seconds of uneven perfection in Montreal. There is no shortage of moments that pull us from our everyday lives into a realm where complexity vanishes and everything seems a little clearer, a little more radiant.

The alchemy need not happen during a headline-making event. It can occur in some out-of-the-way competition. A young high school softball player discovers with one breathtaking catch just how good she will be. A veteran relief pitcher throws through the pain to save a game that keeps his team out of last place. A boy sprints to improve a few places in a cross-country race whose winners finished minutes earlier. The athlete's sublimity does not need a new stadium or an ESPN "top 10" ranking to enter the world. It only needs a competitor breaking the bounds of the possible. And a spectator to watch that happen.

This shamanistic power explains why the athlete rules the Western imagination. He—and, after centuries of being sidelined, she—is without rival as a secular icon. No other figure is the focus of so much passion, controversy, expectation, and disappointment. No other archetype has such a powerful hold on as many dreams. Rappers, rockers, movie stars, politicians, self-help gurus, and talk show hosts all have their constituencies, but none of them have the ability to stop the world in its tracks like the athlete.

This iconic power is not just about on-field performances. It is a fascination that involves more than wins and losses, more than broken records or collapses before the final whistle. For better or worse, we have elevated the athlete to a position that transcends anything he or she might achieve on the field. He has become an archetype for dramas that have nothing to do with athletic competition. We do not simply think about the athlete. We use him as a means of thinking about ourselves.

A champion bicyclist gets cancer and becomes the most inspirational patient in the world. A gifted basketball forward decides to switch teams and sets off a heated debate on racism and loyalty. A sprinter bolts by a frowning dictator and is seen to repudiate an entire evil ideology. A golfer cheats on his wife, and everyone starts talking about fidelity. Two runners raise gloved fists, and a turbulent generation finds its most iconic image. An unknown sledder from an obscure country dies in a crash at the Olympics, and he embodies the tragedy of youthful mortality more visibly than any one soldier perishing in an endless war. Unless, of course, that soldier happens to be a professional athlete. The ability to drain a jump shot or run the 40 yards in 4½ seconds catapults high school students to the front of the increasingly long college admission line and earns them scholarships worth hundreds of thousands of dollars. An entire nation can stake its pride on the performance of athletes, as happened in 1980 during the ice hockey semifinals between Cold War rivals at the Lake Placid Olympics, or in 1938, when Joe Louis and Max Schmeling faced off for the heavyweight crown as their respective nations prepared for war.

This book is an attempt to chart the athlete's course from those early religious rituals to his present incarnation as a ready-made figure for just about any vice or virtue we choose. How he went from shaman to showman. The story has many twists but one recurrent theme—the athlete's ability to represent the ethos of his era. If that story has a Western bias, that is because the athlete who now dominates our world is a Western phenomenon. The stadiums and arenas of North America and Europe are the shrines where any player must now come if he or she wants to be an icon. This includes the Olympics, that traveling circus of immortality, supposedly global but really a product of the West, with nearly all its sports created in Europe or the United States. Cricket on the Indian subcontinent, rugby in South Africa and Australia, soccer in Africa and South America, baseball in Japan and Cuba—for better or worse, most of the games the world plays have origins that are distinctly Western.

Ultimately, the athlete's story is not only about his various incarnations as an icon. It is also about how he has managed to survive them. For all the overwhelming metaphorical weight we place upon the athlete, for all our appropriations of his charisma for commercial purposes, his power to provoke awe has not diminished. For all the disappointment we express when he fails to serve as a role model or political symbol, he continues to be able to freeze the world with his performances, to pull us out of our daily lives into a magical realm where we are once again 10 years old, seeing something that feels as if it is beyond our understanding, but somehow still belongs to us. Try as we will to weigh him down with meaning, the athlete remains one step ahead of us.

CHAPTER 1

BEAUTIFUL DEATHS

On May 16, 2010, the heavily underdog Black Knights men's lacrosse team of the United States Military Academy defeated the defending national champion Syracuse University Orange in the opening round of the NCAA championship tournament. Although it was one of the greatest upsets in the history of the sport, most observers would have been inclined to view the result as the sort of thing that can happen on any given day. Predicting winners and losers is a risky business in any athletic endeavor.

Some players on the West Point team saw something deeper than chance at work, however. Tyler Oates, a senior who was planning to serve in Afghanistan as an Airborne officer upon graduation later that year, told the *New York Times* soon after the game that "we never go on the field saying, 'We're going to give them a heck of a fight,' or 'We're going to play our best' . . . You're not going to go into Afghanistan saying, 'I hope I do all right.' That's life or death, not win or lose, but what makes you think the way you approach a lacrosse game should be different than the way you approach a training exercise or when you actually go to war?"

Whether he knew it or not, Cadet Oates was talking about more than just the preparation and mind-set of his Black Knights team when he hinted that military training could give West Point the edge over their civilian counterparts on the field of play. He was, in fact, describing a relationship between the athlete and the warrior that stretches back to the earliest days of humankind's history. From the first moment men understood they would have to kill in order to survive, they have engaged in games that were designed to perfect these deadly skills.

The athlete was born of the hunt. His first talents were those needed for pursuit and slaughter. There is evidence that *Homo erectus* was using clubs and perhaps even nets to hunt as long as 400,000 years ago. *Homo sapiens* was certainly hunting with spears by 70,000 BC. Their prey included such formidable creatures as saber-toothed tigers and mammoths. Cunning, strength, and swift action would have been essential to make a kill.

These hunters needed to practice in order to sharpen their skills. The best way to fling a net, the proper trajectory of a spear, the ideal pace at which to pursue an animal over long distances— these were things that could best be learned and perfected through repetition. These were the first games, performed in the intervals between hunts. There would have been little sense of play about these early contests, however; a distinct lack of mischief or joy. This was a grim business. It was about survival. Aggression without accuracy would have been worse than useless to the early hunter. Miss your prey and it could flee. Or it might even turn on you.

Performed in a group setting, these hunting exercises would have led to competition. As the German historian Gerhard Lukas claimed in a 1969 study of the origins of athletics, "the first sport was spear throwing." It is easy to envision how this played out. A tribe of Paleolithic hunters would fashion weapons, then test their effectiveness in order to choose which would be best for the bloody business at hand. One man would throw, another would follow. The player who demonstrated superior killing skills would earn a prime place in the hunt, along with all the benefits such status would bring.

The hunt also helped mold the human body into its present form, one capable of athletic feats. As our frames evolved from the pygmy *Australopithicus* of 3 million years ago, the need to run and throw caused our skeletons and muscles to develop in ways that would later allow us to sprint hundred-yard dashes, leap for rebounds, and serve aces. We were built for sports by our early history of hunting. The line from the hunter's club to the Louisville Slugger might be a long one, but it is also unbroken.

As weapons became increasingly sophisticated, more intensive training was required to master them. The atlatl—a cupped shaft used to propel darts—was in use as early as 30,000 years ago. An ancestor of the lacrosse stick and jai alai basket, it could propel a spear with far greater speed and accuracy than an unimproved arm. Modern enthusiasts can fling atlatl darts over a thousand feet at speeds reaching 100 miles per hour. Our ancestors, whose survival was at stake, were probably even more proficient.

But only if they practiced. Put an atlatl into the hands of an unschooled Paleolithic hunter, and you had a hairy man with a stick. Give it to one who had been properly trained, and you had someone who could fell grazing mammals from hundreds of yards away. Practice became even further ritualized once the bow and arrow became part of the hunter's arsenal. The bow has been in use in primitive forms for tens of thousands of years; it had reached its current design in Northern Europe by 8000 BC. Five millennia later, the Mesopotamians were leaving behind fragmentary accounts of archery competitions. At around the same time, the Egyptians were providing detailed frescoes showing that they held not just archery contests but also wrestling matches. Athletic competition was becoming inextricably woven into our cultural fabric.

These contests not only helped tribes hunt. They also allowed them to choose leaders. From the time of the earliest hominids, physical prowess was the primary means of establishing tribal status. Leaders in nearly every culture were the strongest and most aggressive members of their clans. This saw little change as the Paleolithic era gave way to the Neolithic; as hunter-gatherers became herdsmen and farmers. A tribe still needed to be protected. In the Sanskrit epics the Ramayana and the Mahabharata, swordsmanship and archery are depicted as fundamental characteristics of a hero. Egyptian pharaohs confirmed their supremacy through their proficiency as bowmen. A reigning pharaoh was expected to surpass the record of his predecessor in shooting arrows from a moving chariot through a small brass target. While it is unlikely that each new king would have in fact been able to break the Egyptian national record, there does not seem to have been any scribe around who was willing to put these failures down on papyrus.

The first athletic contests were not simply a means of improving skill or establishing a right to rule. They also took on a profound magical importance. Early human competitions were thought to be incantatory. By strenuously acting out the hunt, with one group as Team Hunter and the other suiting up in animal skins as Team Prey, early humans saw themselves to be engaging in sacred rituals. Not only was it thought that such a game would lead to success in further hunts, but most belief systems also held that these mock hunts would bring fertility to a tribe's women, rain to thirsty crops, and cures to the sick. The athlete became a shaman. This ritual aspect of games is seen in cultures from Africa and Asia to Europe and North America. In all of them, it was important that this hunting game be no mere pantomime. Both sides had to strive to win. A powerful performance was needed to satisfy that most demanding of audiences—the gods.

And then there was war, which proved the hunt's equal in powering the rise of the athlete. Growing human populations and periods of scarcity led to bitter rivalry over dwindling food supplies. Hunters became hunted. The Talheim Death Pit in Germany establishes that tribes were engaging in organized battle at least 7,500 years ago; it is likely some form of combat was taking place much earlier. This led to an expansion of the role of athletic contests. Killing a human being was a more complicated proposition than taking down an animal. The boys and young men of a tribe would be encouraged to participate in games of war that would turn them into effective killers. After all, combatants possessing advanced martial skills usually prevailed, while those relying on simple aggression were consigned to the Darwinian flesh heap. These martial games became particularly important as the age of the hunter-gatherer gradually gave way to the era of the farmer, and a man's daily work no longer prepared him for battle. Something was needed to keep his killing skills sharp—war games.

The athlete became the warrior's double. As with those West Point lacrosse players, competitions served as dress rehearsals for war. The cultural historian Johan Huizinga maintains in his seminal 1938 study of the role of play in human evolution, *Homo Ludens*, that in the "archaic sphere of thought . . . play is battle and battle is play." There was no separation between athletic and military skill. Training was the same for both. The only difference came in the fading seconds of the game. The athlete pulled his punches; the warrior followed through. Combat, after all, was usually hand to hand. The man you had to kill was often as close as a blitzing line-backer. You taught yourself to be strong and fast and resilient—or you died.

It should come as no surprise, then, that the first fully fledged depiction of an athletic competition comes from one of the earliest accounts of war—Homer's *Iliad*, written in the 8th century BC. In Book 23, during a lull in the fighting, Achilles requests that his comrades participate in games honoring their slain comrade, Patroclus. The tribute will include chariot racing, boxing, wres-tling, a footrace, sword fighting, archery, and the discus and javelin throws. Precious metals, livestock, horses, and female slaves will be the prizes. Without a moment's hesitation, Greece's greatest soldiers become its most competitive athletes. But this is not rest and relaxation; these men are not simply blowing off steam. Their games are in many ways a continuation of battle by other means. From the very first, the soldier-athletes engage in acts of ruthless cunning and unreserved generosity. The stakes are nearly as high as they are during the war itself.

The chariot race that opens the competition sets the tone for everything that follows. Homer describes it with a breathless attention to drama and detail that would make a modern sports-writer proud. There is even some overbearing coaching, as King Nestor provides his son Antilochus with long-winded advice on how to race. After assuring the prince that "there's no need to issue you instructions," the king, in what would become a time-honored tradition of coaches everywhere, then spends the next 50 lines doing exactly that: reviewing course strategy, listing the strengths and weaknesses of his competition, and even telling Antilochus how he should position his body in the chariot. During the race, the prince proves himself to be his father's son when he rages at his underperforming horses like a football coach trailing by three touchdowns at halftime:

> Why falling back, my brave ones?
> I warn you both—so help me it's the truth—
> no more grooming for you at Nestor's hands!
> The old driver will slaughter you on the spot
> with a sharp bronze blade if you slack off now
> and we take a lesser prize. After them, faster—
> Full gallop—

Despite these blunt commands, Antilochus finishes second, and then suffers the indignity of being accused of fouling other riders. He is stripped of his prize by Achilles, who rules over these games with the steely authority of an old-time baseball commissioner. Threats and appeals ensue, accompanied by the distinct sense that a brawl is about to break out among the competitors. Achilles must use all his powers of persuasion to calm the hot-blooded contestants.

The intensity of the competition remains high through the remainder of the games. Before the boxing match, which Homer assured the reader will be a "painful contest," the boasts of Epeius foreshadow the bombast of many modern fighters.

> I'll crush you with body-blows,
> I'll crack your ribs to splinters!
> You keep your family mourners near to cart you off—
> once my fists have worked you down to pulp!

As predicted, Epeius wins with a devastating punch, then graciously helps his bloodied opponent to his feet. Ulysses employs a more subtle form of psychological warfare during the footrace. Unable to pass Ajax, he calls upon the goddess Pallas Athena for help. In what is perhaps the first instance in Western literature of an athlete rigging a result, the goddess trips the leader, sending him face-first into a dung pile to give Ulysses the victory. A god intervenes yet again in the archery competition. After Teucer, the favorite, forgets to honor Apollo before taking his first shot, the jealous god of archers causes the mortal to miss the quivering dove that serves as the target.

The pitched intensity of the competition here is more than just macho posturing. As with their primitive ancestors, the Greeks are performing not just for each other, or even for any Trojans who might be watching from the ramparts. Their audience is the gods. These are, after all, funeral games. Athletic intensity is intended to impress the heavenly spectators waiting to usher Patroclus into the next world. It is only by competing as hard as possible that these Greek warriors can truly honor their fallen comrade and assure his place in eternity.

The reason behind this belief is a concept that stands at the heart of Greek culture—*arete*. It is a difficult word to define. Valor is perhaps the best translation. Honor, excellence, and bravery also give a sense of its meaning, as does Hemingway's notion of grace under pressure. Or, simply, guts. *Arete* was the most potent motivating force in Greek culture, more compelling than gold or sex or political power. The Greek male was judged by the sum of this quality he earned through his actions. And the primary way to get it was in competition.

For the Greek warrior, battle was not just about gaining territory or riches. It was about showing his comrades that he was brave and honorable. The warrior met his foe on the battlefield and he killed him. He then took possession of the enemy's armor and weapons. By doing this, he assumed his enemy's *arete*, thereby increasing his prestige among his comrades. Achilles was seen as the foremost of the Greeks because he killed Hector and the other Trojans he faced, often in circumstances where lesser men would have been vanquished. Enemy blood was the wellspring of his fame.

The battlefield was not the only place that *arete* could be won. In fact, Greek men saw much of their lives as a competition. Aeschylus and Sophocles gained fame in playwriting contests; Socrates' dialogues and Demosthenes' orations could be downright pugilistic. The main arena for competition beyond the battlefield were athletic games. The one aspect all these contests shared was that there was only a single winner. One man walked away with *arete*. There was nothing noble to be gained from a close second. There were no honorable mentions in Greek culture. This is why Achilles' athletes go at it with such intensity.

Ancient Greece was a shame culture. It was a society that valued winners and had nothing but contempt for losers. Vince Lombardi may have been of Italian ancestry, but he sounded thoroughly Greek when he quipped: "Show me a good loser and I'll show you . . . a loser." A Greek man would do just about anything to avoid being disgraced in front of his fellow citizens. This is why the struggle for *arete* did not always involve fair play. Rules were valuable to the Greek athlete, but not absolute. The stakes were simply too high. Ulysses was not above enlisting outside help, and no one thought ill of him. The only way a loser could be certain to command respect was to experience a *kalos thanatos*—a beautiful death. The *Iliad* is filled with examples of warriors dying nobly, thereby inoculating themselves against shame.

All of which explains why Achilles called for games to honor Patroclus. The races, fights, and throws served the solemn purpose of surrounding the soldier's soul with an aura of valor as it entered "Hades house." They provided opportunities for sacrifice every bit as important as the immolation of sheep or even the horrific slaughter of twelve "splendid" Trojan youths. Just as he dishonors Hector by dragging him through the dirt, so Achilles honors Patroclus by having his men risk shame and display valor.

Athletic prowess was also a sure indicator of nobility among the Greeks, just as it was with the Egyptian pharaohs. During his long journey home after the Trojan War, Ulysses proves himself royal through a simple display of physical skill. After the wanderer washes up on the island home of the Phaeacians, the local king has his men stage an athletic festival as a way of demonstrating their worth to their guest. When Ulysses, bone weary from his long voyage, tries to beg off, the king's son Laodamas encourages him with words that can serve as an epigraph for the entire Greek view of the athlete:

> So long as a man lives, he has no
> Greater glory than what he wins
> With his feet or his hands in the games.

Ulysses once again declines and is taunted by a young punk named Euryalus, who accuses the great warrior of being "not a real man" and then levels one of the most devastating insults in the Greek arsenal: "You don't seem to be an athlete." He might as well have called him a sissy. Ulysses picks up a large discus and throws it so far that even Athena, his protector, is impressed. He then challenges the awestruck Phaeacians to any contest they choose. There are no takers. Ulysses will have another chance to establish his nobility upon his return home to Ithaca, when he dares his wife's suitors to an archery contest, which he wins in the most emphatic manner possible—by killing them all.

The strong association of the Greek athlete with the warrior was to undergo a radical break just around the time Homer was composing the *Iliad* and *Odyssey*. This was due to a new type of soldier who appeared in the 8th century BC—the *hoplite*, or armored infantryman. He was a very different figure than his predecessor, one who would forever change the way the Greeks fought and competed. His name comes from his large oval shield, known as the *hoplon*. He also wore a helmet, a breastplate, and leg cladding. More distinctive than the armor was the fact that the *hoplite* fought in a tight formation called a phalanx, which would slowly advance toward enemy positions, long spears bristling from a metal shell of shields. Short swords were to be used only if the formation happened to break.

Unlike his predecessor, the *hoplite* was not expected to distinguish himself through individual acts of heroism. He was a faceless cog in an armor-encrusted killing machine. Swordsmanship and dexterity were less important than an ability to hold formation at all costs. The individual bravery and innovation that Achilles displayed on the battlefield were no longer the hallmark of a good warrior. Athletic skill would have to find another proving ground to be part of the Greek male's never-ending search for *arete*. It soon did, in a festival that continues to provide one of the prime forums for the athlete to make his name.

WE know a great deal about the Greek Olympic games. We know that they began in 776 BC and ran without interruption for a thousand years, taking place every four years on the second full moon after the summer solstice. We know that the festival was so durable that it was even held right on schedule in 480 BC, even though at the same moment Athens was being torched by invading Persians. We know that the games were held in a remote valley a couple hundred miles southwest of Athens, and that the first event ever contested was a 210-yard race called the *stadion*, which was won by a cook named Koroibos. In fact, we have a record of every winner of that particular race for the next millennia. We know that Plato, who reportedly gave up a wrestling career to become a philosopher, attended the games as an avid fan, as did his student Aristotle, though the playwrights Aristophanes and Euripides thought they were a grotesque waste of time. We know that women could not compete in the games or, in most cases, even attend them. And we know that winners, who would later be held up as model amateurs by the founders of the modern Olympic movement, were often seasoned professionals, able to translate their victories into riches undreamt of by most of their peers.

The one thing that remains a mystery about the Olympics is how they began. It is likely their origins have something to do with religion. Olympia was one of the most sacred spots in all of Greece, a temple of Zeus where the greatest of the gods supposedly wrestled Kronos for the ultimate gold medal—dominion over the universe. (Olympia should not to be confused with Mt. Olympus, which is in the northern part of the country and, as a sporting venue, would probably be amenable only to ski jumping.) Olympia was also the stomping ground of the demigod Hercules, who measured out the distance of the *stadion* for races against his brothers. Gods such as Apollo, Hermes, and Ares were also believed to have competed at this site.

Given Olympia's rich mythical history, it naturally became a locus for pilgrims. The Olympic games probably grew out of the rituals they performed to honor their muscular gods. There was also a secular legend about the festival's origins. In it, the region's king, Oinomaos, announced that he would give his daughter Hippodameia in marriage to any man who could beat him in a chariot race. The only catch was that losers would be executed on the spot. After a number of failures, a young man named Pelops bribed a stable boy to sabotage the king's chariot, causing him to suffer a fatal crash during the competition. Pelops won his bride and a festival was instituted in his honor, proving once again that in Greece it was not so much how you played the game that mattered, but whether you won or lost.

Whatever their precise origins, the Olympic games became one of the key events on the Hellenic calendar, so important that they were used as the basis for marking the dates of famous deaths, battles, and earthquakes. The term *olympiad* means, in fact, "every four years." The athlete became the biggest draw of antiquity. The efforts Greeks put into attending the games were astonishing. Olympia was a remote location, lacking facilities for the thousands who would attended. The fact that the games were held at the height of the Mediterranean summer hardly made them more comfortable. Flies were especially pestilential—one of Zeus' epithets at Olympia was "Averter of Flies."

And yet people came. In a time when the primary means of transportation were sandals, they flocked from hundreds of miles away. They came from Athens and from Sparta, even when these two nations were engaged in deadly conflict. During an era when travel by boat was arduous at best, they came from the islands of Sicily and Crete. Although there is no truth to the legend that a general truce was called for the games, participants were given safe passage through war zones as they traveled to and from Olympia. Writers and musicians were present in abundance, many of them taking advantage of the large cosmopolitan crowd to debut new works. And the nightlife was legendary, with Athenian swells spending small fortunes to set up luxury tents that were the ancient equivalents of skyboxes and tailgate parties.

What people really came to see were the athletes. This was by no means their only opportunity—there were numerous other competitions throughout the Greek world, so many in fact that a top athlete could keep busy the entire year. But there was something special about the games at Olympia. It was here that the athlete became a figure who bridged the gap between the sacred and the secular. Godlike in his aura, he was also very earthly in his sweat and struggles. Greek myths were full of epic contests and examples of heroism; in the Olympic games, people could see them play out before their eyes.

The Greek athlete cut a striking figure. First of all, he competed in the nude. Boxers may have worn *himantes*, crude gloves made of leather straps, and some wrestlers may have practiced infibulation, enclosing their foreskins with leather bands to prevent catastrophe. Despite these minor adornments, the athlete was expected to perform naked. Even jockeys. It would have been a sight made even more vivid by the fact most of them were covered with olive oil. Athletes basted themselves with it so regularly that they carried an implement called a strigil for scraping oil off once it became dirty or rancid. The origin of this nudity is based on an incident in 720 BC when a sprinter named Orsippos of Megara lost his loincloth during a race and yet kept running to victory. The practice probably would have come about without his slip, however. The Greeks loved the beautiful male body, a passion that found expression in media ranging from sculpture to the writing of Plato.

The Greek Olympic athlete was also a professional. The myth that the Greek Olympian was a gentleman amateur is precisely that—a myth, disseminated in the late 19th and early 20th centuries by the upper-class founders of the modern Olympic movement as a way of keeping poor people from competing. There is, in fact, no Greek word for *amateur*—it is a French term from the Age of Enlightenment that means enthusiast or hobbyist. Greek athletes might have competed for glory and the esteem of their peers, but they also were in it for the loot, as Achilles demonstrated when offering prizes of gold and slaves in the games for Patroclus. So deeply ingrained is this tradition that the Greek word *athletes* translates as "one who competes for a prize."

And that prize could be very large. Although the only actual trophy for an Olympic victory was a crown of olive branch cut from a sacred tree at the site, winners could expect to receive the antique equivalent of large endorsement deals for the prestige they brought their native states. The most common reward was a guarantee of free meals for the rest of an athlete's life. Hometowns also knocked a hole in the city wall to allow for a triumphant return, which must have become a headache for places with multiple winners. Top athletes were also able to make fortunes competing in the wide circuit of games that did award prizes of gold and olive oil. These could total the equivalent of millions of dollars. A single victory in the Olympics could set up a runner or wrestler for life.

Greek athletes were specialists. Some were fast. The Greeks were serious about their runners. False starts were punished by whipping. Most everyone knows the legend of Phidippides, the soldier who in 490 BC allegedly died from exhaustion after running the 26 miles from the battlefield at Marathon to Athens to announce the Greeks' victory over the Persians. Although the story is probably apocryphal, it does emphasize the high regard with which the Greeks held runners. In addition to the *stadion*, there were two other sprints, one of approximately 400 meters, and another in which the competitors wore the armor and carried the shield of a *hoplite* soldier. The greatest Greek runner was Leonidas of Rhodes, whose won all three of these races at four consecutive Olympics.

The athlete could also have been strong. Power was tested in the so-called heavy events, whose patron, naturally enough, was Hercules. The javelin and discus throws fell under this category, though fights were the most popular tests of strength. These included boxing, wrestling, and most notoriously, the *pankration*, a free-form style of fighting (its name translates as "all-powerful") that is a predecessor to our mixed martial arts. Only biting and eye-gouging seem to have been forbidden in this event. Legend has it the style was invented by Hercules when he put a fatal choke hold on the Nemean lion during the first of his twelve labors.

The most famous participant in the heavy events, and perhaps the most famous of all Greek athletes, was Milo of Croton, a wrestler from the 6th century BC. Legend has it that as a boy he would lift a calf onto his shoulders every day in order to build his strength. As a man, he was capable of snapping a leather cord wrapped tightly around his forehead by simply bulging his veins. Contemporaries also report that he had the habit of standing on a greased discus and challenging all comers to knock him off. No one ever succeeded. During one opening Olympic procession, he reportedly carried an ox into the arena, slaughtered and cooked it, then ate the entire beast himself. If he was trying to intimidate his opponents, it worked—he won six consecutive Olympic titles in the span of a quarter century, a record unsurpassed during the thousand-year run of the ancient games. In a development that could have been written by a Greek tragedian, his pride also proved his undoing when he decided to test his strength by tearing open a tree that had been partially split by a woodsman. After he moved it a few inches, the wedges fell out and the trunk snapped shut, trapping his hands. As night fell, wolves appeared and feasted on the athlete's richly muscled flesh.

Milo's chief rival for the greatest Greek athlete was Theogenes of Thasos, a boxer and *pankration* fighter who amassed 1,300 victories during the course of a two-decade career. His reputation was so fearsome that many of these wins were uncontested, or *akoniti*, which translates as "dustless." In the course of this legendary streak, he became one of the wealthiest men in Greece, as well as a powerful politician. By the time of his retirement, he had begun claiming direct descent from Hercules. A hero cult was established in his name after his death. Five hundred years later, die-hard fans were still worshipping him.

Fame was not only gained through physical exertion. Rich men with little physical prowess were able to buy themselves a place on Olympia's sacred fields in the *tethrippon*, a thundering four-horse chariot race. In a tradition that would have made George Steinbrenner and Mark Cuban green with envy, it was the owner of the chariot, and not the jockey, who was awarded the olive wreath. The most infamous of these owners was Alcibiades of Athens, a rich politician who used his money and connections to assemble a dream team of horses that won him numerous crowns. He also threw the most lavish parties in the history of the games. We do not know the names of his riders, though it is likely they were slaves.

The flamboyance and influence of figures like Milo and Alcibiades caused some Greeks commentators to criticize athlete worship. Diogenes the Cynic pointed out that even the best human performance could always be bettered by some animal. The scrawniest rabbit could outrun Leonidas, while Milo would have been no match for a rampaging bear. The playwright Euripides, in his fragment *Autolykos*, maintained that training Athenian boys as athletes weakened the national defense: "What man has ever defended the city of his fathers by winning a crown for wrestling well or running fast or throwing a diskos far or planting an upper-cut on the jaw of an opponent? Do men drive the enemy out of their fatherland by waging war with diskoi in their hands or by throwing punches through the line of shields?" It is a persuasive argument, though it should perhaps be taken with a grain of salt, since Euripides was not above writing a victory ode for Alcibiades, work for which he was undoubtedly well remunerated. Another trenchant critique of the athlete came from the physician Galen several centuries later. In *On Choosing a Profession*, he claimed that "athletes do not share in the blessings of the mind. Beneath their mass of flesh and blood, their souls are stifled as in a sea of mud . . . they spend their lives like pigs—over-exercising, over-eating and over-sleeping."

But these dissenting voices were rare. By Greece's Golden Age, the athlete permeated the culture. Poems were written in his honor; he was immortalized in sculptures like Myron's *Diskobolus,* or Discus Thrower, and Lysippos's *Apoxyomenos*, which depicted a tall athlete using his strigil to wipe olive oil from his skin. At the funeral Alexander the Great staged for his general Hephaestion in 324 BC, 3,000 athletes competed to honor the fallen warrior. In addition to the Olympics, there were three additional crown games where victory also brought great prestige and wealth to an athlete. Winners at all four were known as *periodonikai*, someone who had won the cycle (*periodes*) of crown festivals. It was the equivalent of golf's Grand Slam or horse racing's Triple Crown.

The athlete's importance was not limited to organized games. Physical training was a foundation of the educational system. A large number of gymnasia were established to teach young men, known as *ephebes*, the skills and values of the athlete as part of their instruction as citizens. As at the Olympics, exercises were performed in the nude—the word *gymnasion* stems from Greek word *gymnus*, or naked. If a boy was talented, he might even attract the attention of a *paidotribe*, or private trainer, the predecessor of the modern coach.

The gymnasium was also where a Greek boy learned the value of shame. In that institution's homoerotic atmosphere, *ephebes* could be humiliated if they lost a contest in front of the older men who took them as lovers. In Athens, Plato's Academy and Aristotle's Lykeion (Lyceum) were built as gymnasia; the work of both philosophers reflects abiding interest in the athlete. Aristotle, in fact, was something of a statistic freak, compiling and revising long lists of Olympic winners. The gymnasium system found a hardnosed cousin in Sparta, where males between the ages of 7 and 30 would undergo a rigorous, at times brutalizing, rearing known as the agoge. Throughout the Greek world, there was no separation between schooling the body and schooling the mind. There were no "jocks" and "brains." Here the ideal of the scholar-athlete was born, one that would temper the view of the athlete for the next two and a half millennia.

The athlete's most profound role in Hellenic culture was to serve as a hero, a concept far more complex to the Greeks than to us. In addition to being an exemplary person, the Greek hero embodied both god and man. Literally. Hercules, who achieved immortality through twelve highly athletic labors, is perhaps the clearest example of this hybrid. The Greeks believed that the athlete performing at the top of his game could also briefly occupy the rarefied borderland between man and god. Perhaps this is why he always competed alone.

There were no teams in Greek athletics. Competitions pitted man against man. Victory or defeat was on the solitary athlete's shoulders. There were no silver or bronze medals. *Arete* was never shared. Neither was shame.

Because prestige and fame were on the line, athletic competition at Olympia was deadly serious. Despite the festive atmosphere that might surround contests, Greeks did not see the athlete as being involved in play or recreation or even entertainment. It is no accident that the Greek word for competition was *agon*, the root of our "agony." Spectators expected athletes to leave everything on the playing field. If they had to choose between suffering and quitting, they were expected to choose the former. Every time.

This would explain the unrivaled fame of the *pankration* fighter Arrichion. In the gold medal match of the 564 BC Olympics, Arrichion's opponent locked him in a choke hold that threatened to become fatal if the fighter did not submit. Instead, Arrichion latched on to his opponent's foot, dislocating his toe. The other wrestler tapped out just as Arrichion died of asphyxiation. The judges awarded the dead man the olive wreath, whereupon the ecstatic crowd carried the corpse from the arena on their shoulders. In his victory, Arrichion experienced one of the most beautiful deaths in all of ancient Greece. By trading his mortal life for eternal fame, he embodied the Greeks' deepest dreams of the athlete. He became godlike. He became a hero.

For winning athletes lucky enough to survive their matches, this transformation was immortalized on the final day of the Olympics. After undergoing a ritual bath, winners would enter the temple of Zeus. Olive wreaths cut from the site's sacred tree by young boys would then be placed on winners' heads as flute music played and spectators outside cheered wildly. For the Greeks, this moment was an apotheosis, a transformation of man into a hero. The athlete's fame would be secure, in this world and the next.

This thirst for apotheosis finds expression in the work of Pindar, the house poet of the Olympics. His Epinician Odes, or songs to victory, were commissioned by athletes to be performed by a chorus after their triumphs. The opening lines of his sixth Nemean Ode describe a world where the line between human and god can be erased by the athlete's sweat.

> The race of men is one thing, that of the gods is another.
> There is a total difference in power so that we are nothing—
> while the bronze heaven remains the gods' secure seat forever.
> But nevertheless—we can become something like the gods,
> through excellence—excellence of mind or of body;
> even if we don't know from day to day—or night to night—
> what finish line fate has marked for our run.

The crowning moment at Olympia established a model that humankind continues to use to this day, even though people no longer believe in a pantheon of gods who wrestle, run races, and shoot arrows. For us, the athlete's apotheosis comes at Olympic stadiums and in World Series locker rooms; on the pitch at Wembley or center court at Wimbledon. These spaces, not churches or cathedrals, serve as the modern equivalents of Zeus' temple. They are the sites where, every so often, time can be momentarily stopped in the belief that something immortal has just entered the world.

CHAPTER 2

FESTIVALS OF PAIN

The Olympic games were still going strong when Greece was finally conquered by Rome at the Battle of Corinth in 146 BC. In fact, the festival would continue to be held without interruption for the next 400 years. Not that this mattered to the Romans. Although they would absorb many aspects of Hellenic culture, they had no interest in the Greek athlete. His public nudity was repellent to a Roman sensibility that liked to keep its decadence hidden behind closed doors; his lack of weaponry and the minimal number of fatalities during play seemed unmanly to a nation that thought sports should celebrate military violence. Besides, the Romans were already in the process of developing a homegrown athlete, one who embodied the pitiless values of an empire that was using the sword to bring the world under its control.

The gladiator is one of the more troubling products of Western civilization. This icon of savagery and bloodlust did not labor in some flyblown backwater, but rather held center stage in the city where many of the West's laws and customs were forged. Two thousand years ago, in the capital of an empire whose leaders saw themselves as duty-bound to civilize a barbaric world, spectacles of violent death were the hottest ticket in town. Despite Roman apologists who championed the gladiator's value as a religious or political figure, there is no avoiding the fact that the bloody display in which he took part erupted from the same dark precinct of humankind's collective soul as the torture chamber, the snuff film, and the death camp.

And yet we are fascinated by him. We enthusiastically allow the gladiator to serve as one of our most influential athletic icons. From the NFL's helmeted, armor-clad football players to heavyweight boxers slugging it out in Madison Square Garden, modern athletes can be unmistakably gladiatorial. The civic stadiums where today's families gather are modeled upon the Roman arenas in which men, women, and children died horrible deaths. The rhetoric of modern competition often sounds suspiciously like the slogans that echoed through the Colosseum as steel ripped the flesh of 100,000 slaves. Filmmakers like Stanley Kubrick and Ridley Scott depict the gladiator's battles in thrillingly choreographed sequences and beautifully saturated colors. On screen, he is a handsome hero who triumphs before he dies. Even his blood is picturesque.

In reality, there would have been very little that was beautiful or heroic at the Colosseum or the dozens of other arenas scattered throughout the Roman Empire. In them, braying crowds regularly gathered to watch wretched human beings slaughtered with swords, lances, axes, spiked gloves, teeth, and claws. While some of these deaths involved exciting combat, most would have been pathetic in the extreme. Crude executions were common. Few participants who entered these arenas could expect to exit alive. Most were *noxii ad gladium ludi damnati*—condemned to the sword in the amphitheatre. Many badly wounded victims had to be finished off by trained killers who roamed the stadium in grotesque costumes.

Hot pokers were used to determine if a fallen warrior was truly dead; coups de grace were often administered with mallets. Wounds often went septic, leading to amputation or lingering death in hellish subterranean chambers. Victory, if one could call it that, only rarely resulted in freedom. Those who managed to survive the carnage were almost invariably condemned to return to their prison training camps to await another summons to the arena. The fact that the people in the stands were speaking Latin did not make any of this less barbaric.

Many of those who died did not even have the chance to defend themselves. The games provided an opportunity for Rome to rid itself of its unwanted. In the intervals between gladiatorial fights, criminals, prisoners of war, and enemies of the state were put to the sword in gruesome processionals. Forget Russell Crowe or Kirk Douglas—these were shivering, filthy, shackled souls yanked from fetid cells to be butchered in the hot Roman sun. As for the gladiators themselves, most were slaves, *infama*, the lowest of the low, on a level with prostitutes and beggars, held in squalor and misery at training academies known as *ludi*. Mass suicides among them were not uncommon. Spartacus did not rebel because he wanted a better pension plan.

The gladiator was born in death. According to the Romans, it was the custom of the Etruscans, their direct ancestors on the Italian peninsula, to make blood offerings of slaves at the tombs of recently deceased noblemen in the belief that their deaths would ease the passage of the departed to the afterlife. While the Greek gods were satisfied with funeral games well played, their Roman cousins wanted blood. It was human sacrifice pure and simple. The ceremony was called a *munus*, or "duty," to the dead. Eventually, the victims were encouraged to fight, perhaps to give the tribute a more noble tone, or simply to make it more fun to watch. As with the Greeks at Troy, the more strenuous and heroic the competition, the greater the glory that would adhere to the soul of the departed. The difference was that there were no valuable prizes for the winners. Everybody died. The rite was inherited by the Romans and formalized in 264 BC when Decimus Junius Brutus staged the first recorded *munus* at his father's funeral.

From this macabre beginning, the gladiator eventually moved to the center of Roman life. Private sacrificial games became public spectacles, a process greatly facilitated around 50 BC when an ingenious Roman statesman named Curio devised the first amphitheater. He did this by constructing two crescent-shaped theaters back-to-back, and then, while both were filled to capacity, he had them pivoted by a hidden mechanism to create an enclosed space in which gladiators began to fight. The effect must have been more thrilling than anything currently offered up in Las Vegas or Disney World. Arenas grew increasingly larger until, in 72 AD, the emperor Vespasian commissioned one like no other. The result, completed eight years later during the reign of the emperor Titus, was the Colosseum, which seated 50,000 people and immediately became one of the most important sites of the Roman Empire.

Even before the opening of the Colosseum, there was a great expansion of *munera*. Whatever connection these games may have had with religious observance began to be drowned in a flood of pomp and gore. The gladiator became emblematic of the most flamboyant excesses of corrupt emperors like Caligula, Nero, and Commodus. He was also synonymous with Roman military power and global supremacy. Amphitheaters appeared in every precinct of the empire; many of those who fought at the Colosseum were prisoners of war brought back from Europe and North Africa. Animals, used both as predators and prey, were imported from as far away as Asia Minor and Ethiopia.

By the time the bloodthirsty emperor Trajan staged *munera* involving 10,000 gladiators in 106 AD, the gladiatorial spectacle had become a highly ritualized, daylong affair. Mornings would usually be given over to *venatio*, or contests between human beings and wild animals such as lions, wolves, wild boars, and elephants. The hunters, known as *bestiarii*, would range in ability from skilled fighters to abject prisoners who were *damnato ad bestias*, condemned to the beasts. Unlike modern hunting, where all power lies with the human hunter, these contests often derived their entertainment value from the prospect of watching an exotic beast tearing the flesh of a petrified person. Audiences would feel let down if there was no prospect of a victory for the animal kingdom. Imagine a modern deer hunt in which the prey can shoot back. And when the match was one-sided, it was often the beast who was given the upper hand. Bound human victims were sometimes crushed by trained elephants, to the raucous delight of an increasingly hard-to-please crowd. It seems that the only time human victory was assured was when an emperor took to the field. After all, *munera* were intended as a display of Roman power. It would not do to have the head of state suffering a loss. Nero regularly participated in these "hunts." He once famously fought a lion that was so heavily drugged it hardly seemed to feel his sharp spear, which was perhaps not surprising behavior from a notoriously poor sport who had himself declared winner of the *tethrippon* race while visiting Olympia even though he fell from his chariot and failed to finish.

The morning session would also occasionally be given over to *naumachia*, in which the arena was flooded so naval battles could be reenacted, with slaves slaughtering one another wholesale from rival boats. More often, these aquatic spectacles, first staged by Julius Caesar to mark his victory over Mark Antony and Cleopatra, were held in vast purpose-built lakes, allowing casts of thousands to bloody the water as they fulfilled the grandiose fantasies of the sponsoring emperor.

After the morning session, in the heat of the midday sun, a procession of criminals would be led into the arena and summarily slaughtered. The numbers of victims ranged from a handful to hundreds. As the statesman Seneca famously quipped, *Mane leonibus et ursis homines, meridie spectatoribus suis obiciuntur*—"In the morning, they throw men to lions and bears; at noon, they throw them to the spectators." It speaks to the brutalizing nature of the games that this was widely considered a lull in the action, the ancient equivalent of baseball's seventh-inning stretch.

Invariably, afternoons in the arena would be dedicated to the most familiar portion of the spectacle—the gladiatorial duels. A wide variety of fighting styles were on display. Armor and weaponry were often derived from those used by prisoners of war from conquered territories. Two of the most enduring gladiatorial styles were the *Samnite*, with his shield, sword, body armor, and visored helmet, and the *Thracian*, who had a shield, helmet and sword but wore no armor. Also popular were the *retiarius*, who used a net and trident, and the *essedarii*, who fought from chariots. And then there was perhaps the most savage of the fighters, the gladiatorial boxer, who wore the *cestus*, a leather glove that was studded with metal spikes and shards of broken glass.

The rules of the *munus* have become so commonplace as to be a cliché. After a colorful opening parade and a ritual salute to the emperor, the fighters would be matched, usually by drawing lots. It was customary to pair off warriors of different styles. Groups would often fight each other. Sometimes these matches were arranged by the emperor to satiate his taste for the grotesque, such as when Domitian staged a battle of dwarves against women. Whatever the pairings, the gladiators would fight until one combatant was killed or overcome. In the event of the latter, the vanquished would await word of his fate from the spectacle's chairman, known as the *editor*. This was often, but not always, the emperor. If a gladiator had fought particularly well, the editor could grant him *missio*, a pardon that allowed him to leave the arena. Some fights, however, provided no such possibility of relief. They were *sine missione*, "without mercy," or to the death. Fighters who had truly distinguished themselves, usually over the course of a series of *munera*, might be granted a ceremonial wooden sword known as a *rudis* that would serve as a symbol of liberation. If the fighter had not earned the respect of a crowd that could be very sophisticated in its understanding of the gladiator's techniques, then the editor was more likely to shout *Jugula!*— cut his throat—than to extend a downturned thumb. The loser would assume a kneeling position and bow his head so a sword could be driven into the back of his exposed neck. Although an unflinching acceptance of the cold metal supposedly allowed a dignified passage into the next world, there was little that was noble about the treatment of his body, which would be collected by slaves dressed as gods and dragged into a filthy morgue in the bowels of the arena known as the *spoliarium*, where the dead gladiator's weapons and armor would often be fought over by scavengers.

While the details of the spectacle are well documented, what remains debatable is why it was so popular among the Romans. There are numerous theories, many of them contradictory. The most famous comes from Juvenal, the Roman satirist active in the 1st and 2nd centuries AD, the heyday of the gladiator: "There was a time when the People bestowed every honor—the governance of provinces, civic leadership, military command—but now they hold themselves back, now two things only do they ardently desire: bread and games." Although he was referring to the chariot races at the Circus Maximus, his cynical view also applied to *munera*. To his critics, the gladiator was a bloody distraction from a political system that had devolved from a republic into a fully fledged dictatorship, a polity where an emperor's most degraded whims stood as absolute law. It is a criticism that finds a powerful echo in the present day, when some commentators see sports as being noisy, colorful diversions offered to a public that is being exploited by the same large corporations who sponsor the spectacles. In this view, a visit to the Colosseum to watch games backed by the emperor is not much different from paying hard-earned money to spend a Sunday afternoon at a football stadium that bears the name of the bank charging double-digit interest on the very credit card a fan may have used to buy his tickets. The gladiatorial games were not only distractions, according to Juvenal and his followers, but also cathartic lightning rods for the pent-up frustrations of citizens living in a society that was both totalitarian and, for the two centuries following the birth of Christ, largely at peace. With their incessant slaughter of criminals, rebels, and prisoners of war, *munera* were also compelling displays of the power of the Roman state for anyone thinking about mounting a challenge to it.

Emperors were known to pluck enemies from the audience to have them fight and die in the arena's dust.

Of course, the long, popular run of the *munera* shows that critics like Juvenal were certainly in the minority, no more influential than some wisecracking columnist at a modern college newspaper who bemoans the ascendancy of football on campus. More mainstream commentators responded by casting the gladiator as a beneficial force in Roman culture. For them, *munera* played a positive educational role, providing Romans with vivid illustrations of decisive battles in the empire's history and also instilling in spectators virtues like discipline, perseverance, and stoicism. Pliny the Younger claimed that watching gladiators accept their fates "awakens contempt for death and indifference to wounds, since even in the bodies of slaves and criminals a love of glory and desire for victory can be seen." The modern scholar Roland Auguet maintains that there was a widely held belief among the Romans that the deaths of the gladiators held an exemplary moral lesson for the public, demonstrating that even the lowest among them could behave heroically beneath the blade. Religious-minded observers took this viewpoint a step further, casting *munera* as an ongoing form of sacrifice in which the blood of the victims would continually renew the Roman state. The gladiator's standing as a role model was dependent, however, on one important factor—his ability not to flinch when the executioner's sword plunged into his flesh. While the Greek athlete may have achieved his apotheosis with a crown of olive, his most visible Roman counterpart achieved fame only with a necklace of steel.

Whatever their ultimate purpose in Roman society, there is no disputing the fact that *munera* were wildly popular. This is why emperors were so eager to sponsor and attend the games, just as American presidents make sure they throw the first ceremonial pitch to open the baseball season. But, as mentioned, the Roman emperors went one step further by actually participating in the games. And it seems the more depraved and tyrannical the leader, the more eager he was to join the fray. Caligula not only fought in rigged contests but also bestowed huge fortunes on his favorite fighters and, legend has it, even temporarily turned over the reins of state to his favorite gladiator, Eutyches. The emperor also used the games to publicly humiliate anyone he feared might rival him in power or popularity, as described in this passage from the historian Suetonius.

> One Aesius Proculus, a leading centurion's son, was so well-built and handsome that people nicknamed him "Giant Cupid." Without warning, Caligula ordered Aesius to be dragged from his seat in the amphitheater into the arena, and matched first with a Thracian net-fighter, then with a man-at-arms. Though Aesius won both combats, he was thereupon dressed in rags, led fettered through the streets to be jeered at by women, and finally executed; the truth being that however low anyone's fortune or condition might be, Caligula always found some cause for envy.

Other emperors exploited the games just as cynically. Nero, as we have seen, also took part in the games, though only after making sure there was no chance of injury or defeat. But it was Commodus, the most depraved of Roman emperors, who was truly obsessed with *munera*. Perhaps because he was widely believed to be the bastard child of a gladiator, he publicly decreed that he was the reincarnation of the demigod Hercules. In order to back up this claim, he practiced his gladiatorial skills on an almost daily basis. He also took part in more than a thousand *munera*, always careful to use real weapons against slaves who were armed with wooden replicas. He also battled countless animals, most notably a running ostrich he decapitated with an arrow he had purpose-built for the task. Needless to say, he amassed a perfect record; until, that is, he was assassinated in his bath by a wrestler named Narcissus.

Although *munera* were often a forum for emperors to enact their dark fantasies, the games did have a more practical political significance. They gave the Roman people a rare, perhaps unique opportunity to confront their emperor, who otherwise kept as aloof as the gods depicted on the Colosseum's friezes. Although this contact sometimes took the form of direct petitions, there was also a cruder, more boisterous rhetoric involved, with citizens cheering or jeering gladiators who were the favorites of a leader.

Perhaps because of the odds stacked against him, a gladiator could become a deeply popular figure in a society that was more than happy to watch him die. Although they were usually anonymous slaves without any social standing, a few became as famous as any politician or writer, their names popularized in graffiti that can still be found in arenas. Flamma the Syrian was perhaps the most renowned of all gladiators. Four times he was presented with a *rudis*, and yet each time he turned his back on freedom to return to the fray. Carpophorus was a beloved *bestiarius* who was said to have slaughtered bears, leopards, lions, bulls, and even a rhinoceros in his long career at the Colosseum. Some gladiators could even grow rich in their profession. According to Suetonius, Nero presented the gladiator Spiculus with a fortune as great as those given generals who had won famous victories over the state's enemies.

The gladiator was also a figure of intense erotic fascination. Tales abound of noblewomen sneaking into gladiatorial quarters for romantic assignations. The most famous of these liaisons is described by Juvenal, who tells of the highborn Eppia leaving her comfortable life with a noble husband to follow her love, the veteran gladiator Sergiolus. Juvenal's less-than-flattering description of the fighter suggests that the athlete's blinding seductive power was already in force:

> This dear boy had begun to shave a while ago,
> and one arm,
> Wounded, gave hope of retirement; besides,
> he was frightfully ugly,
> Scarred by his helmet, a wart on his nose, and his eyes
> always running.
> Gladiators, though, look better than any Adonis...

Certain aristocratic men, perhaps seeking to secure some of this sexual charisma for themselves, enlisted to fight in *munera*. Others did it to escape creditors or simply because they were seeking thrills. The practice became so widespread that there was even a name for freeborn men who willingly condemned themselves to this life of hardship and probable death—*auctorati*.

The gladiator was by no means the only popular Roman athlete. In terms of sheer quantity of fans, he was surpassed by the charioteer, who raced in front of crowds of 250,000, or roughly one quarter of Rome's population, at one of the largest sporting venues in human history—the Circus Maximus. By all accounts, the races were intensely competitive. As many as twelve chariots would thunder around a track that was over 600 yards long. Races would comprise fourteen laps around the two large pillars at either end of the stadium. Needless to say, congestion at tight turns made strategy and ruthlessness every bit as important as speed. As with contemporary NASCAR races, many people came just to see the pileups, known as shipwrecks. Deaths were not uncommon. A racer who could cause a shipwreck and then escape unscathed would be assured fame, at least until the next pileup. Causing a wreck in front of the emperor's box was particularly well received. The greatest of all Roman charioteers was Gaius Appuleius Diocles, a former slave who would amass a staggering 1,462 wins before his retirement. The driver Hierocles, a former slave whose great athletic skill was complemented by striking blond good looks, caught the attention of the emperor Elagabalus, who was so besotted with the charioteer that he took him as a lover and began to call himself "the Queen of Hierocles." By most accounts, the horseman wound up running the empire from behind the scenes, like his predecessor Eutyches. It was only when Elagabalus tried to have his lover named his successor as emperor that the nobles had had enough. Both men were executed.

As in Greece, the real fame and power in the races went to the horse owners. Rival stables, signified by the colors worn by charioteers, became the first athletic teams. While these colors were originally nothing more than a randomly assigned means of differentiating horses, they soon took on powerful political associations.

In a template for countless crosstown rivalries to come, the Blues became the team of the city's aristocratic elite, while chariots from the Green stables represented the great unwashed. Caligula, whose contempt for the nobility was so great that he once tried to have his favorite horse knighted, spent a lot of time in the Green stables in order to endear himself to the hoi polloi.

Despite the immense popularity of the charioteer among the Romans (and his resurrection in the film *Ben-Hur*), it is the gladiator who lives on in our imagination and serves as a basis for our conception of the athlete. This raises troubling questions. Why does this doomed, murderous slave continue to intrigue and even inspire us, when he should by all rights be consigned to history's dungeon along with the Indian killer and the storm trooper? Why does a figure so deeply steeped in sadism and blood continue to influence our conception of the athlete every bit as profoundly as Achilles, Ulysses, and Milo? One answer is that the gladiator represents competition at its most intensely focused. He is the archetype for every athlete who faces impossible odds and yet still refuses to quit. While we can appreciate a tennis player with an unreturnable serve or a soccer team with an impenetrable defense, we reserve a special regard for the athlete who competes with courage and resolve even when victory is impossible. The gladiator inhabits a small, ephemeral world, bounded by the vastness of death and defeat, and yet within this crushing space he continues to compete as if he is playing for worldly fame and riches. He knows that there is nothing for him outside the arena but slavery and extinction, that his lowly status means that he will probably be forgotten before his body has even started to cool. So he transforms the competition into life itself. His entire existence crystallizes into the moment when swords clash. The gladiator lives for only as long as he competes, and yet in those few moments he lives more purely, more intensely, than any spectator in the Colosseum, even the emperor. This is why we continue to value him. More than any other figure, he reminds us of the athlete's ability to perform with the utmost passion and dignity even as the clock runs out on him.

The gladiator also reminds us of the complicated pleasure that can be derived from an athlete's pain. People like to watch violence. Not all people, of course, and not all kinds of violence. But one need only glance at the box office numbers for gruesome horror films or tabulate Internet hits for graphically violent video clips to understand that some deep part of the human brain thrills to the sight of bloodshed. The athlete provides us with one of the most socially acceptable means of experiencing this vicarious carnage. Millions of spectators pay to watch championship boxing matches on cable television because they like to see the devastating collision of fist and jaw; the NHL refuses to ban fights because watching players bloody one another is an essential part of the spectacle. Rigorous efforts have been undertaken to make football safer since its murderous days at the beginning of the 20th century, yet nothing will ever rid the sport of the core violence that comes from having powerful men run into one another at top speeds. The reason is simple: if football ever were to be defanged, it would become as popular to watch as Ultimate Frisbee. Attempts to strip the athlete of his warrior origins seldom work. The most popular new sport of the past decade is mixed martial arts, whose violence harks back to a time many thought was long gone. The gladiator, at least in the form we imagine him, is nothing more than the grandfather of these various figures. When it comes to enacting violence, the modern athlete remains very much the child of the slaves of the Colosseum.

And it is not just a talent for inflicting pain that we admire in the athlete. It is his ability to take it. We want the athlete to be able to experience levels of pain and fatigue that ordinary human beings could never endure. Athletes are avatars of suffering, and no one encapsulates those qualities better than the doomed gladiator. There is a deep, perverse pride in his oath: *uri, vinciri, verberari, ferroque necari*—to be burnt with fire, shackled with chains, whipped with rods, and killed with steel. We expect a boxer to be able to throw a devastating uppercut, but we also reserve a special adulation for those who can take a punch. And we love the wide receiver who can bounce up after taking a big hit every bit as much as the linebacker who delivers it. One of the most exhilarating moments in Olympic history came at the 1976 Montreal Games when the Japanese gymnast Shun Fujimoto performed on the rings even though he had broken a bone in his leg during an earlier routine. Although he could have easily retired from the competition, he wanted to give his team the chance to win their fifth consecutive men's title. His solid routine turned into a legend when he was able to remain upright after his twisting dismount, his face only barely registering what must have been indescribable pain.

While only psychopaths yearn for an athlete's death or permanent injury, many fans expect them to bear pain on a scale we would not accept in our daily lives. Filmmakers understand this. In two very different boxing movies, *Raging Bull* and *Rocky*, we see two very different characters, Jake LaMotta and Rocky Balboa, triumph over opponents even though they lose big fights. They achieve victory by taking a beating and remaining on their feet.

They are gladiators who do not flinch as they receive the coup de grace. As Robert De Niro's Jake LaMotta, his face a bloody mess at the end of a stinging defeat, says to a bemused Sugar Ray Robinson: "You didn't get me down, Ray."

And it is not just in accepting violence that we demand this sort of stoicism of the athlete. It can occur even in sports where pain is self-inflicted. A world-record mile run would not be complete without the winner's face clenching into a mask of agony as the tape is broken. No sight better captures the ecstatic beauty of athletic fatigue than the collapse of spent rowers at the end of the annual Boat Race between Oxford and Cambridge. The Czech long-distance runner Emil Zatopek is one of the most appealing athletes of all time, and an important part of his charisma is the fact that his face was usually a rictus of suffering when he raced, even as he was winning gold medals and setting world records. In his autobiography, the cyclist Lance Armstrong perfectly captures this intimate relationship with pain. "Cycling is so hard, the suffering is so intense, that it's absolutely cleansing. The pain is so deep and strong that a curtain descends over your brain. . . . Once, someone asked me what pleasure I took in riding for so long. 'Pleasure?' I said. 'I don't understand the question.' I didn't do it for pleasure. I did it for pain." For most people, this sort of statement would seem like the sort of sentiment that might require some serious time on a therapist's sofa. Coming from a top athlete, it perfectly encapsulates a mind-set we celebrate. We not only expect the athlete to stoically accept the figurative sword to the back of the neck. We want him, on some level, to find redemption, even victory when the curtain descends.

The gladiator could never outlast the empire he helped define.

The *munera* went into rapid decline in the late 4th century, after the Christian emperor Honorius shuttered the gladiatorial academies, thereby choking off the supply of fresh combatants for the Colosseum. It is hardly surprising that it was a Christian who brought the games to an end, since members of that rapidly growing religion had provided fodder for the ravenous maw of the munera ever since they started to be seen as a threat to the Roman state. The phrase "thrown to the lions" may be a stale cliché for us, but there is no doubting its immediacy and terror for the thousands of members of St. Paul's congregation who were slaughtered in the arena by lions, dogs, swords, or fire.

Honorius' edict was not simple revenge, however. Christianity, with its denigration of earthly pursuits, proved fundamentally antagonistic to not just the gladiator, but the athlete in nearly all of his embodiments. Its sights set on heaven, the Catholic Church had no time for displays that celebrated the body. During the five dark centuries that followed the collapse of the Roman Empire, no iconic athlete emerged. Chariot racing remained popular in some locales for a few centuries after the gladiatorial arenas went dark, especially in Asia Minor, where Porphyrius of Constantinople became the greatest charioteer of antiquity. The sport took a serious blow in 512 AD when a barely comprehensible 30,000 people died in riots following a race in Constantinople. The popularity of chariot racing could not be sustained against growing ecclesiastical belief that it was a damnable frivolity. It would be left for another figure, one even the Catholic Church could not deny, to return the athlete to the center of the Western imagination.

CHAPTER 3

FIELDS OF GOLD

In the summer of 1520, two of the most powerful men on the planet met in the French countryside to discuss the future of the world. On one side was the French king, Francis I, 25 years old and celebrated for his learning and patronage of the arts. Considered his nation's first Renaissance ruler, he was so close to Leonardo da Vinci that he was believed to have cradled the great artist's head in his arms as Leonardo drew his last breath. Joining Francis for this epic meeting was a figure of even greater stature—King Henry VIII of England. An accomplished scholar and composer, Henry was also a remarkable athlete, skilled at archery, wrestling, tennis, bowls, and of course, jousting. At 6 foot 2, he towered over most of his subjects, even many of his generals and knights. His palace, Hampton Court, could be mistaken for a sprawling sports complex, complete with tennis courts, bowling greens, and a magnificent jousting arena. Even without the accoutrements of office, Henry would have been considered one of the most formidable men of his era.

The reason for the meeting could not have been more serious. The two monarchs were trying to forge a military alliance between their nations in order to avert the prospect of a damaging European war. Francis was particularly eager for a pact, since he needed England on his side to counter the threat from the Holy Roman Empire under Charles V. The importance of the meeting was underscored by the fact that both kings brought retinues that were too large to be accommodated in any existing castle. Instead, they met just outside the port city of Calais, draining swamps, razing hills, and setting up great tents to create an ad hoc city worthy of the occasion. Henry's "palace" alone was a 12,000-square-yard tent so complex that it contained a central courtyard with two fountains that flowed with red wine. His tent and those of his nobles were decorated with silk fabric laced with gold, leading the summit to be dubbed the "Field of Cloth of Gold."

Although grave diplomatic business was being conducted, the meeting quickly took on a festive atmosphere. Lavish banquets and concerts, attended by lords and ladies whose costumes contained as much gold cloth as their tents, took place every night. The days, meanwhile, were given over to a series of athletic contests. While royal sports such as archery, falconry, and bowls were on offer, the most intense competition came in the jousting. As detailed in Hall's Chronicle, published less than thirty years after the summit, the noblemen took their games every bit as seriously as they did their negotiations. The jousting tournaments were especially dramatic. At a designated hour, the two teams, led by their kings, entered a vast, carefully prepared playing field. The competitors wore ornate armor that had been specially crafted for the occasion. Henry's horse, for example, was decorated with 2,000 ounces of gold and 1,100 large pearls. The Earl of Devonshire and his men were dressed in armor embellished with silver as well as gold. Although Hall does not describe the French in quite such detail, it is safe to assume that the Gallic knights would have been eager not to be out-peacocked by their English counterparts.

All this frippery did not cover faint hearts. The competitors on both sides were the fiercest, most highly trained athletes of the day. The competition was intense and, in one final instance, may have helped change the course of history. Both kings seemed to have acquitted themselves well. In their many jousts against each other, Henry maintained a slight edge, though Francis more than held his own against his larger and more experienced opponent. Recognition should also go to the Earl of Devonshire, who lost his jousting series with Francis by a score of 3 to 2, but did manage to break the French monarch's nose in the process.

The decisive moment in the summit came when Henry challenged Francis to a wrestling match. The smart money would have been on the powerfully built Englishman, but Francis stunned everyone by throwing Henry for a clear win. According to French accounts, Henry was none too happy with the loss. The games were abandoned; negotiations broke down soon after. No major treaty was signed. The following year, Henry formed an alliance with Charles V and joined him in attacking France, leading to a bloody five-year war that engulfed much of Europe. There is no report of Henry ever wrestling the Holy Roman Emperor.

Although the idea of, say, Nixon and Khrushchev donning leotards and grappling at the height of the Cold War is not without a certain appeal, the fact that two world leaders squared off in pitched athletic contests during the course of a crucial geopolitical summit will strike most modern readers as bizarre in the extreme. But to Henry and Francis, nothing could have been more natural. By trying to knock each other off their horses with long wooden lances, they were merely behaving like most European aristocrats of their era. Athletic feats, particularly jousts, were how noblemen had been gaining recognition, establishing rank and demonstrating character for the previous 400 years.

After a long absence, the athlete finally regained a central place in the Western imagination with a figure that has become as familiar, some would say as clichéd, to us as the gladiator—the medieval knight. By the 12th century, this mounted, armored warrior, whose original role was to maintain order at home and conduct holy wars abroad, was established as the most important athletic icon in Europe. Men such as Sir Giles de Argentine, John Astley, and Ulrich von Liechtenstein were the sporting superstars of their era, their accomplishments carefully recorded by historians and breathlessly celebrated by troubadours. The festivals in which they participated were wildly popular at a time when there was little else to divert people. By some contemporary accounts, as many as 40,000 knights showed up at a tournament held in Mainz in Germany in 1184; of the thousands who attended the Tournament of Neuss, also in Germany, in 1241, no fewer than 60 died from injuries received while competing.

Despite the Catholic Church's belief that the body was a vessel of sin and that something as trivial as sports just might lead to damnation, this new-style athlete has his roots in Christianity. The knight came into his own during the First Crusade in 1099, when a few hundred mounted noblemen were able to capture Jerusalem by using coordinated lance charges. (Their peasant comrades, taking part in a campaign known as the People's Crusade, proved far less fortunate: lacking armor and operating on foot, they were slaughtered by Turkish archers outside of Constantinople.) Inspired by this success, knights began to gather in order to practice mounting these attacks. These assemblies, known as hastiludes or "games of lances," originated in France but spread rapidly to Britain and Germany during the 12th century. Before long, they became formalized into tournaments in which prizes were awarded and, more importantly, standing at court was determined. Religious devotion, political dexterity, and scholarship might be useful tools to the ambitious young knight, but nothing could help him climb a royal court's greasy pole more quickly than a display of prowess on the field of play.

The first hastiludes were very different from our modern image of a pair of jousting knights thundering toward each other in an enclosed stadium, cheered on by an audience that included royalty, heralds, and nubile women. Instead, the first tourneying knights participated in something known, appropriately enough, as a melee. On an appointed day, competitors would gather in a remote field or section of forest, often situated in the borderlands between two rival nations. The English-Scottish border was a particularly fertile ground for tournaments, as were the hotly contested frontiers of Brittany and Normandy. Participants would divide into two teams, a home side known as the tenants, and visitors known as the venants. These teams were composed not only of knights but also retinues of foot soldiers who were ready to assist their masters once the action started. Occasionally, no teams would be chosen, and the melee would simply be conducted as a free-for-all, with every man for himself. These were relatively rare, however. Like the wars they so closely resembled, these tournaments were normally about one clan establishing supremacy over another.

The hastilude would begin with a set piece in which two leading knights would square off for a preliminary duel that would be conducted both on horseback and on foot. The results of these were not binding. It was conducted merely to set the day's tone and get the blood of the young knights up. Once this violent prologue had reached a conclusion, the melee itself would begin. The action was barely distinguishable from battle. Teams would conduct charges en masse, or knights would break off for individual duels. Participants would remain mounted until they had been forced from their saddles, whereupon the action would continue on foot.

There were, at first, no restrictions on the sorts of weapons that could be used. Knights deployed everything from lances and broadswords to crossbows and daggers. Nor were the weapons necessarily blunted. The object was simple—to take an opponent captive, then collect a bounty before releasing him. Ideally, this could be accomplished by simply unhorsing him, though proud, hot-blooded young knights, fighting for their honor, were not always easily corralled. The action could become intensely violent. Death tolls among the participants could be higher than those registered in actual battles featuring the same number of warriors. There was collateral damage as well. Farmers unfortunate enough to live near the melee often saw their crops and livestock destroyed. Peasants literally had to lock up their daughters. Anyone stumbling into the midst of one of these early tournaments could have easily thought himself caught up in an actual war.

Not surprisingly, these rowdy gatherings soon became unpopular with the authorities. Although the knights saw themselves as soldiers of the Cross, the Catholic Church issued a series of bans on tournaments. This was due not only to the general carnage and disruption, but also to the Church fathers believing that a knight's time could be put to better use invading the Holy Land and slaughtering infidels. Kings, meanwhile, were not happy about large groups of armed noblemen gathering outside of their supervision. In addition to the wasted energy and lives, the possibility for insurrection was simply too great.

But boys will be boys, and the knights would not be denied. The urge to perform athletic feats needed an outlet. So kings, most notably Richard I of England (1157–1199), decided to accommodate the tournaments by giving them the royal seal of approval. This led to some profound changes in the way knights competed. The prospect of hundreds of armed noblemen rampaging through the countryside was clearly not a circumstance most kings were eager to sanction. Also, the knights themselves were discovering that the prospect of gaining recognition from their peers—and, perhaps even more important, impressing young women—was next to impossible in the wide-ranging rustic chaos of the melee.

And so, during the 13th and 14th centuries, tournaments evolved into the form we now know, in which individual knights faced off against one another. The action moved into enclosed areas called lists, which were bordered by grandstands known as *berfrois*. The joust, which became even further stylized in the early 15th century with the introduction of a barrier meant to prevent horses from colliding called the tilt, eventually became the principal means of competition. A joust could be contested with either a sharpened lance or one blunted by a fitted cap known as a coronal. Victory was achieved by splintering a lance against an opponent's armor and, ideally, knocking him from the horse. If a scoring system was being used, blows to the head were more valuable than shots to the torso. A hit was registered only when the attacker's lance splintered against armor. Death might not have been the goal, but it was a fairly common outcome. In addition to the crushing wounds and broken necks that could come from falling from a galloping horse while wearing a suit of iron, splintered lances had a habit of finding a way through chinks in the armor, especially of the helmet. The most famous jousting casualty was King Henry II of France, who died of septicemia in 1559 after his eye was pierced by just such a broken lance as he tilted against the Scottish captain Gabriel Montgomery.

The joust was not the only means of combat in a tournament. A multistage event known as the feat of arms was also popular. This comprised a progression of styles that were agreed upon beforehand. The rules to an individual feat could be complex, detailing the various types of permissible weapons, the progression of fighting styles, and even the number of allotted blows. A match usually began on horseback. After a number of jousting passes, the knights drew broadswords and used these to try to knock each other from their saddles. Competitors would then dismount to continue to fight on foot. Axes, daggers, and maces would be deployed. Submission was the principal means of determining a winner, though heralds, elderly knights, and even the king could be drafted in as judges for hotly contested matches. Needless to say, fatalities were not uncommon in this style of mixed martial arts, with exhaustion being high among the causes of death.

Because this was the Age of Chivalry, when conduct and communication were governed by a strict code of manners, challenges were issued with a formality that belied the savagery of what was to come. When Philip Boyle of Aragon agreed in 1438 to meet the British knight Sir John Astley, one of the era's most feared tourneyers, Boyle's letter gives little sense to the modern reader that the men would soon be clubbing each other with broadswords.

> Be it so that I, Philip Boyle, Knight of the Realm of Aragon, was charged to fight with a knight or with a squire to serve my sovereign lord the tres excellent and tres puissant Prince the King of Aragon and Castile, that I might not be delivered from my said emprise for the accomplishment of them in the realm of France, therefore I have come to the realm of England and into the court of Prince of the High Majesty the very high, lustrous, and victorious Prince the King of England and of France, the chief of honor, valor and prowess, seeking supplication and grace . . .

Despite being spattered with this opening salvo of persiflage, Astley was judged the winner of the duel, which contemporary illustrations suggest was settled with poleaxes. He was awarded a knighthood on the spot by King Henry VI, a prize that in this case came with a sizable yearly income. As athletes have learned from ancient Greece to the present day, one big win could set a man up for life.

Besides the movement from the open field to the enclosed stadium, the other key development in the medieval tournament was a movement away from aggressive combat with actual weapons, known as combat *à outrance,* to competitions *à plaisance,* in which blunted weapons were used to conduct duels that had more to do with theater than warfare. There were a variety of reasons for this evolution. On the most basic level, kings were simply losing too many courtiers to injury and even death. Also, with the rise of infantry and especially the introduction of firearms, the need to train knights to do actual battle became less urgent.

Although battle with sharpened weapons remained part of the tournament right up to the time of Henry VIII, by the 1400s there had begun a marked trend away from the tooth-shattering, head-splitting melee of the 12th century. Like the Super Bowl and the World Cup, tournaments became increasingly spectacular. Many were themed, with knights dressing up as Antony and Cleopatra, the Pope and his Cardinals, or the Seven Deadly Sins. Among the most popular role-playing tournaments was one in which knights, in a medieval equivalent of NFL football players wearing throwback jerseys, would perform in the costumes of mythical Arthurian knights such as Lancelot, Gawain, and Galahad. In these gatherings, known as Round Table tournaments, as much energy could be expended on dancing and feasting as on hastiludes. Perhaps the ultimate example of the movement from combat to display came when jousting knights began to use a ring as a target instead of a rival's chest or head. What started out being a competition in which injury or even death was possible had become more akin to a circus or pageant.

This movement away from violent combat brought an inevitable evolution in the knight's most characteristic feature—his armor. The first tourneying knights wore extremely heavy suits of thick iron whose overriding purpose was to ward off the blows of sharp weapons. But these proved to be too unwieldy for crowd-pleasing displays of martial skill. Crucially, they also made it difficult for ladies in the stands to decide which was their favorite knight. A more manageable and attractive suit was devised, consisting of a layer of tough leather known as *cuir bouilli*, which was then covered by linked steel rings, or mail. Plated metal provided an outer layer. While the first helmets were crude, bucket-like cylinders with narrow eye slits, these were later given duck-billed grates that could deflect sword tips and splintered lances from the eye slits. In keeping with the movement toward spectacle, armor would often be adorned with colorful tokens that were provided by the unmarried women who were among a tournament's most ardent spectators. A popular knight could wind up with nearly as many embellishments as a race car at Indianapolis or Daytona has decals.

Who took part in the hastiludes? What sort of man went to the considerable expense and very real danger of donning unwieldy armor so that he could engage in a contest that risked serious injury and death? First of all, he was a member of the nobility. Most had been dubbed a knight by the king and were usually employed in the service of a lord. Others were squires looking for a means of achieving knighthood. Whatever their particular circumstances, any blood spilled in tournaments was blue. The skills and virtues expected of a knight were those of the court, not the peasantry. While there is some evidence that commoners took part in a variety of footraces and ball games during the Middle Ages, it is inconceivable that a lowborn person would don armor unless he had already been elevated to the aristocracy by the king himself.

This knight was also a soldier. Until the advent of firearms, the first and foremost military training on offer in Europe could be found in melees and lists. As with Achilles' games for Patroclus, many tournaments took place during war, particularly at sieges, when there could be long intervals between battle. And the line between the hastilude and actual combat was often blurred. Scores were often settled, lethally, under the guise of the tournament. Occasionally, tournaments provoked full-scale battles, especially when fought between nations like England and Scotland, who bore little love for one another in first place. It is not hard to imagine how a fragile truce might have been shattered between two warring fractions who came together to play at combat, especially after a serious injury or death occurred.

The feat of arms also became a means of settling legal disputes that could not be resolved in a court of law. In a process known as chivalric combat, a direct ancestor of the duel, two knights would do battle with a variety of unblunted weapons until one was killed. The survivor would then be judged to have the law on his side. If one of the knights was in any way incapacitated during the course of the contest, this was deemed an admission of guilt. He was immediately executed. In "The Knight's Tale" of *The Canterbury Tales*, Chaucer provides an example of such a judicial combat when Palamon and Arcite, two young knights contending for the hand of the beautiful Emelye, are forced by Duke Theseus to fight a melee in a large, purpose-built stadium to determine who will be the successful suitor. Although Theseus sternly decrees that there are to be no deaths in the fight, only one of the principal combatants survives.

The tourneying knight became a deeply romantic figure. This is hardly surprising, given the drabness and difficulty of much daily life during the Middle Ages. A decorated, armored figure galloping at full stride on a richly adorned horse would have been a deeply compelling sight. He also would have been very intimidating, which is why lords put him to use collecting taxes and quelling peasant uprisings when he was not busy trying to impress the ladies in the list.

But there was more than just showmanship at work. The knight expressed some of the core values of his feudal European society every bit as deeply as the Olympian encapsulated the ethos of ancient Greece. He was without doubt the most vivid embodiment of chivalric code that ruled the nobility during that time. The conduct of these athletes of the cross, at least in theory, became the ideal to which all gentlemen were urged to aspire. The virtues of bravery, steadfastness, service to the poor, and devotion to women were believed to be housed in his armor. Put in modern terms, he became the era's primary role model. Priests and monks might have pointed the way to heaven; the knight exemplified how to live on earth.

The tournament also provided proud, energetic young noblemen with a rare opportunity to woo eligible young women. Adorned with decorations signifying his beloved, he could perform in a manner intended to demonstrate his ability to protect a potential bride in a society where unmarried females were usually in grave risk of rape and abduction. In a time when the barriers between young men and women of the aristocracy could be all but insurmountable, the knight's display of athleticism became a primary means of erotic interplay between the sexes. It also provided women with a rare sense of empowerment, since they were often able to set the standards a knight must attain in order to win her hand in marriage. She would sometimes set the bar very high indeed, leading to the creation of the most charismatic athletic figure of the era—the knight-errant.

In a time when most knights served one specific lord, these

wanderers acted like free agents, in constant search of opportunities to establish their prowess and, by extension, their virtue. (*Errant* does not here mean "in error," but rather roving in search of adventure.) This did not mean, however, that they were in it for themselves. The knight-errant had a master. She just happened to be a mistress, a young unmarried woman who had publicly spurned the knight, then sent him on a lengthy mission to prove himself worthy of her love. In doing so, she often set a number of victories he would have to attain before he could return to her. Athletic competition became a means of accumulating marital stock.

A knight-errant's modus operandi was simple. He would arrive in a locale and post a notice challenging all comers. Men such as William Marshal, who once fought so furiously that he had to place his head on an anvil to have his helmet removed by a blacksmith, began to make names for themselves through their skill. In a time where the most common media was word of mouth, they become mobile advertisements for themselves. Their arrival would cause court life to come to a halt as young knights suited up to prove themselves.

Although only a few noblemen actually won their wives by "going errant," they were the ones who got all the ink. The most famous of these wandering knights was the Austrian jouster and poet Ulrich von Liechtenstein, who was born around 1200. (Although Heath Ledger's character in the frothy Hollywood movie *A Knight's Tale* bears Ulrich's name and some of his attributes, relatively little in this tale relates to the historical figure.) The real Ulrich combined the martial ferocity and romantic sensitivity that were the hallmark of his class. Spurned by the woman he had loved since he was 12, he dedicated his life to winning her back on the field of play, a quest he detailed in his chronicle *Frauen-dienst*: "In the Service of the Ladies." Proudly bearing tokens of his love, he wandered from town to town, from tourney to tourney, taking on all comers in an effort to build up a record of courage and valor that would eventually win her over. This quest reached a sort of fever pitch when he spent a month fighting in the guise of Venus in order to demonstrate his commitment to love. His record in drag was 307 to 271. And yet still his lady spurned him. It appears that, in the 13th century at least, a .531 average was not enough to win a damsel's heart.

With characters like this wandering the land, it was inevitable that the knight would become one of the most important protagonists in the era's literature. His greatest chronicler was the 12th-century French poet Chrétien de Troyes, who is never better than when he depicts knights in battle or at play. In his romance *Cliges*, de Troyes vividly illustrates the centrality of the tournament in medieval life. The eponymous hero, a teenage Greek prince, secretly falls in love with the German princess Fenice while visiting her court with his uncle, the Greek emperor. The bad news for Cliges is that his uncle also loves the young beauty. In order to impress her, Cliges challenges the nephew of yet another suitor to a joust, so that he might tilt "strenuously for her before the eyes of all, only that she may hear that he is valiant and very skilful; for in any case it would be meet that she should esteem him for his prowess." He proves victorious, though it is not enough to win her over. Later, he puts his martial skills to more urgently practical use while rescuing her after she is kidnapped by the rival clan whose member Cliges earlier defeated.

Yet even these heroics are not enough to win Fenice, who

decides to hold out until her suitor's stock has risen even higher. It is only when Cliges goes errant and visits the court of King Arthur, the Olympics of tourneying, that he proves his worthiness to be a husband to the beautiful princess. There he takes part in a mega-tournament that pits him against three of the greatest knights of his day: the fearsomely named Sagremors the Lawless, the rather less impressively titled Percival the Welshman, and the dashing Lancelot of the Lake. He wins all three feats, earning a shot at the greatest of all knights, Sir Gawain. They fight fiercely, though the match ends in a draw when King Arthur stops the contest, fearing that he is about to lose two of his greatest warriors. Only after compiling an unassailable record of bravery, after having "wrought many a knightly deed," does Cliges feel confident enough to return to his Fenice and rescue her from his corrupt uncle.

Although most modern competitors and fans share neither his chivalric code nor his religious fervor, the knight persists as a powerful athletic archetype. On its most basic level, this esteem is easily understandable. The image of armored warriors thundering toward one another on decorated, lathered horses is as deeply compelling as gladiatorial combat, only without the explicit barbarism. But there is something else that attracts us to this figure, something entirely new to him. With the knight-errant, the athlete becomes *sentimental*. While the ancient Olympian and the gladiator were not lacking for ferocity and courage, it is difficult for the modern observer to imagine either displaying an excess of feeling. The Olympian is as affectless as the marble statues we now know him by, while the gladiator represents a cruelty that is the polar opposite of sentimentality. With the lovelorn knight-errant, however, emotion inspires athletic activity, while victory on the playing field leads to the triumph of romantic love. With the knight, the athlete no longer simply competes. He *feels*. An echo of this sentimentality can be heard in the first question asked in nearly every post-game interview with an athlete currently broadcast on television—*how does it feel?*

For all his flamboyance and emotional intensity, the knight was finally brought down by something Ulrich and Cliges probably knew nothing about—gunpowder. With the advent of firearm-wielding infantry, the tournament was no longer an effective means of training soldiers. And in a time when there were fewer obstacles to intimacy between the sexes, jousting also became an inefficient way to woo women. Far better to use poetry and song at close quarters. The knight began to fade from the scene. During the Renaissance, virtue moved indoors. Sports became a leisure activity. It would be a long time before another influential iconic athletic figure emerged.

CHAPTER 4

THE ROUGH AND THE FANCY

In December 2007, Michael Vick, the gifted quarterback for the Atlanta Falcons, was sentenced to 23 months in prison for his part in staging illegal dog fights at his Bad Newz Kennels in Virginia. Vick would also receive a 3-year suspension from football for his crimes, thereby forfeiting tens of millions of dollars in salary and endorsement deals. What shocked so many fans was not that Vick had been charged with a felony. Being placed under arrest, after all, is not exactly unheard of among professional athletes in the early part of the 21st century. It can sometimes even be seen as a badge of honor. Rather, what was so deplorable was the nature of the offense itself. In addition to forcing dogs to take part in horrific fights, Vick and his associates routinely killed those who did not perform adequately. Methods of execution included hanging, electrocution, drowning, or simply slamming the defenseless animal against the ground.

It is a mark of the evolution of sporting values that a person who had engaged in similar activity to Vick's just a few hundred years earlier would not only have avoided arrest or even censure, but may also have found himself in the most fashionable of company. During the Renaissance and the Age of Enlightenment, cruelty to

58

animals was not only accepted, it was one of the most popular types of spectator sport. In England particularly, watching dogs, bears, or cocks battle to the death, often in circumstances designed to maximize the combatant's suffering, was seen as perfectly legitimate of a pastime as watching tennis or golf is in our day. It was even acceptable for royalty to engage in these shows. Queen Elizabeth 1 was fond of attending "baitings" in which ferocious dogs such as mastiffs would be loosed upon a bear that had been chained to a pole. Bear gardens were often located next to theaters so that people looking for a day's entertainment could take in both shows. Some scholars believe that Shakespeare saw these spectacles as a threat to his box office, which is why he inserted a bear, somewhat incongruously, in *The Winter's Tale*.

An era that got its sporting kicks from the recreational slaughter of animals was always going to find it difficult to produce an athletic icon representative of the culture's core values. Although games and athletic spectacles became increasingly popular during the period ranging from the late 16th to the early 19th century, no single sporting figure on a level with the Greek Olympian, the gladiator, or the tourneying knight arose to fire the imaginations of his contemporaries. While the Renaissance and Enlightenment produced a broad array of iconic figures in disciplines ranging from portrait painting to theoretical physics, the athlete became noticeable by his absence.

There are a number of reasons for his disappearance. One of the most important was the relocation of courtly virtue from the jousting arena to indoor locations like the library, the conservatory, and the council chamber. The young nobleman was no longer expected to prove himself through athletic endeavor. The knight gave way to the courtier, who relied on wit, manners, diplomacy, erudition, and artistry to make a name for himself. *The Book of the Courtier*, published in 1528 by the Italian diplomat Baldassare Castiglione, advised the would-be gentleman to quickly master physical skills such as fencing and riding, then put them aside for more serious pursuits like rhetoric, poetry, and the study of Latin. Athleticism was by no means disdained, but it was seen as slightly less valorous than proficiency at speaking, dancing, or painting.

Another reason for the vanishing of the iconic athlete was the rise of the explorer. Every era needs a dynamic figure to spark its imagination, and the sailor setting out for a mysterious and potentially punishing horizon proved a perfect fit for the Renaissance mind. Adventurers such as Columbus, Magellan, and Raleigh moved dynamically through space and time, displaying the sort of bravery and charisma that in other eras would have belonged to the athlete, just as astronauts could rival baseball players for supremacy in the American imagination in the 1960s. Renaissance explorers also found favor at court much more easily than they would have done had they focused their energy on jousting, competing in fencing competitions, or honing their tennis games. If an ambitious young man was looking to make a name for himself, he was more likely to do it at sea than in the list.

The rise of Puritanism also contributed to the athlete's decline. To the followers of Luther and Calvin, sports were seen as frivolous, profligate, and ultimately sinful. Play was the Devil's business. While the Catholic Church's opposition to the tournament was ultimately halfhearted, the Puritans were unrelenting in their hostility toward participation in sports, as either an athlete or a spectator. Games played on Sunday were particularly obnoxious to them. The stern Puritan leader Philip Stubbes, in his 1583 treatise *The Anatomie of Abuses*, equates athletes with actors in their venality. He seems particularly incensed by folk football, a rowdy early version of soccer. Calling it a "bloody murthering practise," Stubbes wanted to know if this is "an exercise for the Sabath day? is this a Christian dealing, for one brother to mayme and hurt another?"

In 1618, King James I sought to settle the dispute between Puritans and his games-loving gentry by publishing the *Book of Sports*, which attempted to delineate what aspiring athletes would be allowed to do on Sundays. The result was an uneasy compromise that did little to appease either side. Archery and many types of dancing were permitted, for example, while bear-baiting was forbidden. Upon taking power during the English Civil War, the Puritans publicly burned the book and then sought to stamp out most athletic competition and recreational games. This campaign was carried out with special zeal among emigrants to New England. Although some recreational activities were allowed in the Massachusetts Bay Colony and other New World outposts of rectitude, they first needed to be proven to increase productivity or piety. The notion of organized games played for pleasure was anathema. As difficult as it now is to believe, there was a time when the city of Boston did not support its local teams.

The disappearance of the iconic athlete was not just a question of fashion and politics. There were also deep philosophical reasons at work. In a time when the newly emancipated power of reason was being celebrated, the idea that athletic performance could be indicative of a man's inner worth was increasingly difficult to sustain. There was little reason to enlist figures such as Lancelot and Ulrich von Liechtenstein to serve as the measures of a man when Leonardo, Shakespeare, and Newton were available. As the leading sports historian Allen Guttmann suggests, the relative lack of interest in the athlete on the European continent during the 18th century, particularly when compared to present-day excitement during soccer season or the Tour de France, stems from the fact that so much energy was being expended meeting the intellectual demands of the Age of Reason.

The absence of an iconic athletic figure did not mean that there was no interest in sports. In fact, a remarkable variety of games were being played. They just did not mean all that much to people. Although the tournament had faded, the nobility continued to participate in leisure activities like falconry, hunting, and fencing. Perhaps the most definitive aristocratic contest of the era was real tennis, an early version of the current game. It was considered to be the "sport of kings" every bit as much as horse racing. Played indoors, it resembled racquetball in its encouragement of shots off the "penthouse" roofs above spectator galleries. It had become so popular by the end of the 16th century that there were 250 courts in Paris alone. Shakespeare references the game in *Henry V* when, before the Battle of Agincourt, the Dauphin, or French Prince, sends Henry a gift of tennis balls as a means of taunting him. Henry acknowledges the joke, but then sends a message back to his French rival that "this mock of his / Hath turn'd his balls to gun-stones" that the English will use to create "a thousand widows" among the French.

Sports were also common among the peasantry and artisans. It is likely that games like folk football and wrestling had been widely practiced during the Middle Ages, though little hard evidence remains of the exact nature of these pursuits. Troubadours, after all, kept their eyes focused squarely on the people who paid their bills—the nobility. We do know that by the 16th century nearly every European community outside the sway of puritanical leaders practiced some sort of ritual folk game. In central Italy, communities around the city of Florence formed 27-man teams to play Calcio Fiorentino, an early ancestor of soccer. Contested in a large sandy field, the object of the game was to throw, punt, or stuff a ball into a small goal. The game was notable for its mayhem, with kicks and punches deemed a perfectly acceptable part of the run of play. There are no records of any superstars, although slumming members of the Medici clan and several future popes were said to have played. Participation seemed to be the point; glory for a victory was shared by the particular community a team represented.

The same can be said for the rough-and-tumble folk football, also known as Shrove Tuesday football, England's precursor to soccer, which so irritated Puritan leader Philip Stubbes. Players could number in the hundreds, so that even the best athlete would be lost in the crowd. This unruly game, which alarmed the authorities every bit as much as the melee once did, would normally pit two neighboring villages against one another. Teams were made up of just about anyone who wanted to play. Games started at a midpoint between the two towns. The object was to propel an inflated pig's bladder by any means possible into the opponent's town center and through the front door of the parish church. Carnage was widespread. The game resembled nothing more than civic unrest. In fact, it had more in common with what occasionally happens on the terraces of English soccer stadiums than the game that is now played on the pitch.

As mentioned, horse racing became extremely fashionable during this period among all classes. In fact, by the 18th century it had become the single most well-attended sport in England, Europe, and the United States. Crowds of close to 100,000 could gather to watch races at Epsom Downs outside of London. Fox hunting also grew widely popular in the late 18th century, with the Master of the Hunt becoming a powerful figure whose authority often trumped individual property rights in rural communities. When a human athlete did manage to achieve fame, it was more as a curiosity than as an exemplar of deeper virtues. Such was the case with the long-distance runner. People did not aspire to be like him. They simply came to watch him compete. In England, the running footman, or lackey, became one of the best-known competitors from the 16th to 18th centuries. In a time when the horse-drawn carriage was the principal means of vehicular transportation, a footman would be hired to run alongside the vehicle in order to clear the way of obstacles, push the carriage when it became stuck, or keep it from tipping over on particularly rough roads. He could also be sent ahead to secure his master's lodging. Needless to say, these men developed endurance skills that would rival those possessed by modern marathoners. The most famous of them was an Irishman named Langham who, in 1583, ran 148 miles in 42 hours to fetch medicine for his noble employer's wife. By the 17th century, gentlemen began to pit their footmen against one another in races that were the occasion for intense wagering. Winnings were rarely shared with lackeys, who had just run dozens of miles, however. In an era when the horse was the most popular athlete, it is perhaps not surprising that human competitors were often treated little better than animals.

By the end of the 18th century, the running footman had vanished, literally unable to keep up with better-made carriages that were moving ever faster along higher-quality roads. Footracing continued, however, with a sport known as pedestrianism, another direct predecessor of modern long-distance running. There did not seem to be much differentiation between walking and running, as long as the pedestrian kept moving. Although races often pitted man against man, and sometimes included women, the central fascination seems to have been to see how far and fast the individual athlete could travel under his own power.

The first famous pedestrian was Foster Powell, a Yorkshireman who would regularly ambulate the round trip from York to London, a distance of roughly 400 miles. His record for this circuit was five and a half days. Perhaps the greatest pedestrian of all was the Scottish nobleman Robert Barclay Allardice (1779–1854), known to his followers as Captain Barclay. He reportedly once walked 72 miles between breakfast and dinner (which must have been a late meal). His greatest achievement came in 1809, when he walked 1 mile every hour for 1,000 consecutive hours, an exploit which attracted over 10,000 spectators. During the reign of Captain Barclay, pedestrianism became enormously popular among a public whose interest in the competitor remained primarily statistical. While the average citizen might know the names of the best pedestrians and even follow his exploits in an increasingly popular press, there was never any sense that they saw him as being a role model. They did not care about his personality or demand to know how he felt. They simply wanted to see what kind of numbers he could rack up.

While pedestrians were able to compete with at least an aura of respectability, a great many athletes, as well as their followers, went underground during the period that lasted from the reign of Queen Elizabeth I through the enthronement of Queen Victoria. Instead of an icon of bravery and rectitude, the athlete became an outlaw figure, associated with the gross excesses and dissolute lifestyles of those who came to watch him. Spectators who found amusement in the cock-fighting pit and bear garden came to view sports as a means of indulging their baser instincts rather than their better angels. A passionate interest in games and contests could often be a sign of moral breakdown. Take the case of the infamous Mad Jack Mytton, the son of an extremely wealthy Shropshire family who can now be seen as the quintessential decadent sportsman of the early 19th century. After being bounced out of two elite boarding schools, the second ejection coming after only three days, Mad Jack somehow managed to finagle his way into Cambridge. Given the fact that he showed up for his first day of classes transporting roughly as much alcohol as the average American fraternity member goes through in four years, it should come as no surprise that he failed to graduate. Never one to be discouraged, upon returning home he bribed his way into Parliament, yet attended only one session before retiring from politics, claiming that he found it boring.

Discovering himself a man of leisure at the ripe age of 24, Mad Jack spent the remainder of his short life indulging his love of sports, particularly horse racing, upon which he gambled away most of his fortune. It was as a hunter, however, that he truly lived up to his nickname. He fed steak and champagne to his best dogs and let his favorite horse live in his large manor house. He also once bit a mastiff whose performance in a fight displeased him, and went rat hunting in the winter with a pack of stable boys, all of whom wore ice skates. (The boys, not the rats, though the thought of putting skates on rodents may well have crossed Mad Jack's mind.) He rode a pet bear to dinner parties and once steered his horse to the second floor of a local hotel, where he proceeded to jump from the balcony. In Paris, he deliberately set his shirt on fire—while wearing it—to cure himself of the hiccups. Throughout these exploits, he drank eight bottles of port a day. Not surprisingly, he died before his 40th birthday while an inmate of a debtor's prison. Although an extreme case, Mytton proved representative of an era when there was little ennobling about an interest in games and athletes.

The sport most closely associated with dissolution and the underground during this time was boxing. In retrospect, this reputation seems unfair to the boxers of the "bare-knuckle" era of the 18th and 19th centuries, many of whom were consummate professionals, if not downright gentleman. In fact, the boxer was the era's only true embodiment of the athlete as we now know him, a figure who was able to perform with skill and bravery while also capturing the spectator's imagination. It was the audience that was the problem.

Although evidence from Egypt and Mesopotamia suggest that prize fights have been held since at least the beginning of recorded history, the first modern boxing match appears to have been staged in 1681. It was sponsored by the Duke of Albermarle. That aristocratic imprimatur was no fluke. Although horse racing, hunting, and real tennis were the official sports of the upper classes during this era, boxing became an increasingly popular destination for slumming lords eager to see how the other half bled. "The Fancy," as these high-betting, slang-talking aficionados were known, became one of era's most fascinating subcultures.

Like so many pioneering athletes, the initial boxing champions were British. The first acknowledged titleholder was James Figg, who won the crown in 1719. He was followed by Jack Broughton, whose main contribution to the sport came after his retirement, when he introduced the first set of rules governing conduct in the ring. These covered such matters as what constituted a foul, the size of the ring, the duration of rounds, and the function of "seconds." Broughton also founded a famous boxing academy, where he was able to teach a wide array of students, many of them from the upper classes, by using "mufflers," or primitive boxing gloves. In an advertisement Broughton took out before opening his gym's doors in 1747, the former champion clearly had the worried parents of young lords in mind when he claimed that his academy would be:

> For the instruction of those who are willing to be initiated in the mystery of boxing, where the whole theory and practice of that truly BRITISH art, with all the various stops, blows, cross-buttocks, &c. incident to combatants, will be fully taught and explained; and that persons of quality and distinction may not be debarred from entering into a COURSE OF THOSE LECTURES, they will be given with the utmost tenderness and regard to the delicacy of the frame and constitution of the pupil, for which reason MUFFLERS are provided that will effectually secure them from the inconveniency of black eyes, broken jaws, and bloody noses.

For the next hundred years, a colorful string of boxers fought under Broughton's system, until it was replaced in 1867 by the

Marquess of Queensberry rules, which mandated the use of gloves, set time limits on rounds, regulated ring size, outlawed clinching, and generally tried to tame this wild sport. Perhaps the most striking of these fighters was Daniel Mendoza, known simply, and not always affectionately, as "The Jew." Relatively small in stature (there were not yet weight classes in boxing) and sporting long curly hair, Mendoza possessed lightning reflexes and a ring savvy that allowed him to defeat much larger opponents. His religious identity was troubling to many, however, leading to perhaps the first "great white hope" fight when he was pitted against Richard Humphries, whose nickname, "The Gentleman Fighter," has less to do with his manners than his religious affiliation. Mendoza won that fight, though he finally met his match when a fighter named John Jackson figured out how to neutralize the mobile Mendoza by grabbing his hair and pummeling him into submission.

While boxers could be earnest if colorful professionals, the crowd that gathered ringside was usually composed of debauched fanatics who brought the sport into disrepute. Very rich men spending an evening at the fights could place wagers of thousands of pounds on a single bout. Drunkenness was so common as to be almost de rigueur; prostitutes and pickpockets were actively trying to get into the breeches of wealthy patrons. George IV was a notorious fan, particularly in his days as Prince Regent after his father suffered a bout of debilitating mental illness. It was, in fact, during his regency that boxing became so popular among both the upper classes and impoverished East Enders that the period came to be known as a time of Boximania. The poet Byron was as avid a follower of the sport as Norman Mailer would be 150 years later. Known to mix it up himself if the opportunity presented itself,

Byron took lessons from the champion Jackson, at whose gym he could be joined by the Prince Regent and many other members of the aristocracy.

Boxing began to permeate the culture in ways few sports ever had. Members of The Fancy communicated via a slang known as flash, which became as important a means of entry into the inner circle of the cognoscenti as the argot of the jazz and rock-and-roll demimondes would be during following century. Use of words like *nobbins*, which meant the money thrown into the ring for the winner after a match, became a sign that the user was a member of select club that excluded all those of a puritanical temperament. As Kasia Boddy points out in her incisive *Boxing: A Cultural History*, this slang even infiltrated the canonical work of writers such as De Quincey, Hazlitt, and Thackeray. In Byron's *Don Juan*, it is said of a robber who is shot by the hero that he:

> . . . was once a kiddy upon town,
> A thorough varmint, and a *real* swell,
> Full flash, all fancy, until fairly diddled,
> His pockets first, and then his body riddled.

The most famous account of this heady era was *Boxiana; or, Sketches of Ancient and Modern Pugilism* by Pierce Egan, first published in 1813 but updated numerous times over the next few decades. It was Egan who provided boxing, that "peculiar trait of the brave natives of England," with one of its more lasting nicknames when he called it "The Sweet Science of Bruising." Containing evocative sketches of such worthies as Dutch Sam, West-Country Dick, Davis the Milkman, and Payne the Butcher,

Egan's work is a milestone in our appreciation of the athlete. His sketch of Jackson at an exhibition staged for the crown princes of Prussia captures the breathlessly laudatory style of the first great sportswriter.

> The elegance of his positions, the celerity of his attack, the fortitude of his manner, and the superior mode he developed of guarding his frame from the attacks of adversaries, created a lively interest among the royal warriors. His symmetry of figure and fine muscular powers, also, did not pass unnoticed.

Things began to change for boxers, their fans, and athletes in general once young Queen Victoria took the throne in 1837. Gradually, the decadence and excesses of the aristocracy and intelligentsia were swept away, replaced by the crusades toward social reform, moral hygiene, and empire building that would come to characterize Victoria's long reign. The athlete was swept up in this cleansing tide. Gradually, he came to be seen not as a sideshow freak or entertaining curiosity, but rather as the embodiment of the core values of his civilization, as he had in ancient Greece, the Roman Empire and medieval Europe. Although the change was by no means sudden or absolute, he began to shed his status as an outlaw, evolving by the end of the century into the very model of what a proper gentleman should be.

CHAPTER 5

MENS SANA IN CORPORE SANO

O n September 7, 1892, two boxers met in New Orleans for a
fight that not only determined the heavyweight championship
of the world but also served as a vivid illustration of the athlete's
transformation from a pariah into an icon of mainstream values. In
one corner was the outlandish champion, John L. Sullivan, sporting his trademark handlebar moustache and the "Long John" leg-
gings that had been named after him. Sullivan had been champion
for ten years, during which time a rapidly expanding popular press
had turned him into America's first nationally famous athlete. His
victories not only had been chronicled in the widely read sensation-
alist magazine *Police Gazette* but also were broadcast almost instan-
taneously by the country's vast telegraph system.

Like so many boxers of his day, Sullivan was of Irish Catholic
descent and had not exactly been given a leg up by a society in
which immigrant Irishmen were widely reviled. This only further
enhanced his mystique, as did the fact that he had risen through
the boxing ranks in an era when prizefighting was illegal in most
states. Early contests had usually consisted of him staking out a
position in a tavern or barn and offering $50 to any man who
could last four rounds with him. His larger matches were held in

clandestine locations such as a Hudson River barge and a remote section of mosquito-infested Mississippi forest. Sullivan's unmistakable image, bare fists raised, could be found hanging on saloon walls and hidden in the bedrooms of idolizing boys. Fans would know all about his famous 1888 bout with the Englishman Charlie Mitchell in France, which lasted for two hours in the freezing rain and was called a draw after both men became so bloody and exhausted that they could not proceed. They would also have been able to read of his 1889 fight against Jake Kilrain, held in secret to avoid interference from the authorities. Sullivan won that brawl after 75 savage rounds.

Challenging Sullivan for the championship was James Corbett of San Francisco. Everything you needed to know about how deeply Corbett differed from the champion could be learned from his nickname—Gentleman Jim. He had attended college, had worked as a bank clerk, and most crucially, had been taught to box by a coach, not by neighborhood toughs out to rob his pocket money. Well-spoken and sporting the sort of pompadour haircut that might be seen on a Yale man, Corbett had a reputation for employing a scientific, methodical style that set him apart from most of his contemporaries, notably Sullivan, who relied on raw strength and aggressive "bull rushes" to win.

The fight was remarkable not only because it matched two athletes of such drastically contradictory temperaments. It also marked the first time the heavyweight championship was contested under the Marquess of Queensberry rules that had been established to civilize boxing 25 years earlier. These were based upon the simple dictum that "no holds barred is not the way." The emphasis was no longer on free-form violence, but on fair play and sportsmanship. Among the new rules were the ten-second count after a knockdown to allow the stunned boxer to recover, a ban on clinching, and most important, the use of gloves to protect the fighter's hands and head.

To the surprise of just about everyone, Corbett won the fight with a 21st-round knockout after exhausting his hard-charging opponent with fleet footwork and punishing jabs. While there were rumors that the hard-partying Sullivan had simply run out of steam, Corbett's victory was mostly seen as a triumph of style and cunning, with the well-coached college boy taking down the graduate of the school of hard knocks. The gentleman had beaten the brute. Boxing had begun its slow transition into the mainstream.

The Sullivan-Corbett fight was a major step in the rehabilitation of the athlete, a process that had been going on for over fifty years by the time the two men stepped into that Louisiana boxing ring. Taking place primarily in Britain and the United States, this journey took the athlete from his shadowy netherworld into the bright day of bourgeois respectability. By the beginning of the 20th century, he not only would have become tolerable in the eyes of the once-skeptical authorities, but would be considered an archetype for the very best Western civilization had to offer.

It was a movement that had its origins in the rise of the machine. The rapid escalation of the Industrial Revolution in Britain and the United States, especially its creation of an ascendant middle class, created conditions that made the mainstreaming of the athlete inevitable. One need only look at the faces in the crowd to mark the change. Before the Victorian era, the people who turned out to watch sporting spectacles had often been an uneasy mix of plebeians looking for relief from lives of hardship and aristocrats seeking escape from social rigidity. Gambling and violence were the only bonds holding them together. Boxers and jockeys could best provide them with the thrills they desired.

The middle-class audience demanded a very different sort of athlete. They wanted a figure who expressed their values: hard work, modesty, integrity, and sobriety. Gambling, public brawling, and animal cruelty were not just distasteful to the emerging Victorian bourgeoisie. They were the explicit targets of high-profile reform campaigns. Someone who supported the aims of the newly created and widely popular Royal Society for the Prevention of Cruelty to Animals could hardly be expected to go watch a cockfight for fun, any more than a temperance advocate would attend a prizefight in the back room of a saloon.

The prime breeding ground for this new model athlete was the English public school, places like Harrow and Westminster, Eton and Rugby. Until the ascension of Victoria, these schools—which were not public at all, but rather exclusive and expensive—served primarily as strongholds for the nation's aristocracy. Despite this pedigree (or perhaps because of it), behavior among the students could be appalling. Teachers and headmasters exercised little control over their privileged charges. Social order was instead maintained by a vicious system of "fagging," in which younger boys would be virtually enslaved, often sexually, by upperclassmen. Drunkenness, gambling, and public belligerence were commonplace, even among students who had only barely reached puberty. The curriculum was a stultifying succession of Latin and Greek lessons, without anything the modern reader would recognize as extracurricular activities.

Things began to change when newly enriched members of the nation's manufacturing class began sending their sons to these elite public schools in the middle part of the 19th century. While they craved the prestige such institutions could confer, these self-made men also expected the schools to reflect their own values. Fagging might be tolerated as a means of instilling discipline, but it was made clear that drunk, slothful 13-year-olds were not part of the program. Headmasters came under immense pressure to reform. Although not all of them were happy about it, they came to see sports as the only way of controlling all of that adolescent energy. Some of the games that were to dominate Britain for the next 150 years were either devised or codified at the nation's elite schools and universities during this time. Rugby was invented at the private school of that name in 1823, while the rules of soccer were formalized at Trinity College, Cambridge, in 1848. Although cricket had been played in various forms since the 16th century, it too became increasingly integrated into school life. By the middle of the century, sporting activities were seen as instrumental in curtailing a student's worst excesses, from disobedience to masturbation. In 1864, a commission that had been set up to study public schools concluded that athletics taught young Englishmen how "to govern others and to control themselves."

Out of this movement grew a new kind of athlete—the British amateur. Although the phrase *amateur athlete* now suggests something of a dilettante, it is hard to overstate how important this ideal became in Victorian England. The amateur was seen to embody fundamental British virtues, especially when it came to managing the nation's rapidly expanding empire. Although the Duke of Wellington's famous remark that "the Battle of Waterloo was won on the playing fields of Eton" was probably apocryphal, plenty of Victorians took it as gospel for how they should set their priorities. For them, courage and teamwork not only helped an Englishman win games. They also prepared him to govern the nation at home and rule the colonies abroad.

Another saying came to dominate the view of the athlete in the second half of the 19th century: *mens sana in corpore sano*, or "a healthy mind in a healthy body." Previously, Christian tradition cast sports as a harmless waste of time at best, and a fast track to damnation at worst. No one, especially an individual with a Puritanical mind-set, would have dreamed of upholding athletic endeavor as a means of instilling virtue in a young person. Now, however, athletic training was seen as a vital feature in the creation of righteous youth. Part of this new attitude had to do with advances in medicine, which were demonstrating the practical value of exercise in maintaining health and prolonging life. Another key factor was the rise of the complex set of theories and beliefs that would come to be known as Social Darwinism. In essence, this view claimed that natural selection took place not only on a biological level but also among social systems. Only the strongest cultures, philosophies, and economic systems survived. The only way white capitalist Christian Britain would prevail against the forces of barbarism and darkness was if it brought its "A game" to the geopolitical playing field.

This belief system had powerful implications for the role of athletic training. If life truly was about the survival of the fittest, then it made sense to get fit. Struggle and selection, after all, are core values on the playground. Mastering them would prepare the boy for manhood in this brave new world of free enterprise and foreign conquest a lot better than learning how to decline Latin nouns, recite Shakespeare, or play the oboe. While athletic training came to be seen as an essential basis for professions ranging from industrial management to the clergy, it was most valuable as preparation for service in imperial institutions like the East India Company. Sports built the sort of muscle required to shoulder what would come to be known as the White Man's Burden. Learning how to be an athlete, in body and mind, trained the British boy for the task of running a distant, hostile outpost, where action and teamwork skills developed on the playground were preferable to anything you could pick up in the classroom.

Given this strong emphasis on sports, a new figure began to emerge in the schools—the "blood," a domineering upperclassman who translated his prowess on the increasingly vast and well-tended school playing fields into hegemony over his peers. Shirt untucked beneath a colorful waistcoat, trailed by a retinue of adoring underclassmen, he was the swaggering paragon of what the school had to offer. And as he graduated and moved on, his values began to dominate society at large.

The gentleman amateur was born. An athletic establishment that was once thoroughly professionalized and geared toward the gambling spectator became the realm of vigorous, virtuous men who were, at least in theory, interested primarily in fair play. For most Englishmen, certainly those of the aristocracy and upper middle class, sports was a means to an end. Few, if any, of the bloods who dominated Rugby or Eton would have dreamed of turning pro as their American counterparts might do a century later. This transformation could be seen in the world of boxing, where the British Amateur Boxing Association was founded 1880 with the motto "Box, don't fight."

While the rise of amateurism was ostensibly about championing a certain sort of Englishman, it was also intended to help exclude another type from the centers of social power. If the amateur who played sports to improve his character was seen as an ideal, then the working-class laborer who competed to make money became anathema. At times, this prohibition could be unapologetically explicit, such as when the nation's premier rowing event, the Henley Regatta, stipulated in 1879 that "No person shall be considered an amateur oarsman or sculler . . . who is or has been by trade or employment for wages a mechanic, artisan, or laborer." The mere fact that an athlete used his hands to make a living was enough to disqualify him from elite competition.

This is not to say that members of the British working class stopped participating in sports. In fact, their exclusion from the ranks of the amateur allowed them to colonize certain sports and infuse them with values considerably different from those espoused at Eton and Oxford. Professional boxing, for example, remained largely the province of boys from impoverished neighborhoods such as London's East End and Glasgow's Gorbals. No sport, however, became a better home for "ungentlemanly" athletes than soccer. Although its rules had been cemented at Cambridge, by the end of the 19th century it was unlikely that many of the best British soccer players were on the verge of being offered leadership positions in the foreign service or safe seats in Parliament. The game had instead begun to take on the aspects of hard-bitten play and rowdy spectatorship that would define it in the coming century.

European nations did not share the British enthusiasm for the athlete as a civilizing force. In fact, sports on the continent took on a decidedly recreational aspect during this era. People hiked, climbed, and skied more for pleasure than competition. Perhaps the most popular example of the recreational nature of athletics was *turning*, a German form of group gymnastics. It was developed in the early 19th century by the Prussian educator Friedrich Ludwig Jahn, an ardent nationalist who thought that rigorous exercise could restore German pride after its defeat by Napoléon. The sport he came up with consisted of large groups of devotees gathering in open spaces to perform a series of synchronized workouts. Nobody kept score. The idea of an individual *turner* distinguishing himself was not only unlikely, it was abhorrent. Participation was the point. The movements of the individual athlete took on meaning only if they were performed in lockstep with many others. Jahn was, in fact, deeply skeptical of British sports, believing that its focus on winning would inevitably lead to a breakdown of social cohesion. By the end of the century turning festivals had become so fervidly patriotic that it is now hard to see them as anything more than ominous precursors to the Nuremberg rallies of the 1930s.

One rare European who was most assuredly not skeptical of the British amateur athlete was a buoyant French educator named Pierre Frédy, Baron de Coubertin. This seemingly unassuming aristocrat was to play a leading role in the definition of the athlete as he entered the 20th century. Eager to reform physical education in France, Coubertin decided to study the British system. The decisive moment in his development came during a visit to Rugby in 1883, where he studied the methods of the famously robust former headmaster, Thomas Arnold, one of the towering figures in the amateur movement. What Coubertin saw and heard convinced him that his mission in life was considerably more significant than improving the way French boys did jumping jacks. He would instead use sports to change the world. Basing his approach on the English gentleman amateur, whom he deemed the very model of "athletic chivalry," Coubertin came up with a wildly ambitious plan to revive the Greek Olympics. This new festival would be a forum for bringing together athletes from throughout the world to engage in wholesome competition dominated by a spirit of fair play. As Coubertin stated with characteristic bombast, the Olympics would "exercise over the sports of the future that necessary and beneficial influence which shall make them the means of bringing to perfection the strong and hopeful youth of our white race."

His plan was based upon a very large fallacy. Thanks to the work of scholars such as David C. Young, we now know that the Greek athlete was never an amateur. As we have seen, even when he competed in games that did not directly offer monetary rewards, he was subsequently provided with a wide variety of benefits that made him very rich indeed. Despite its lack of historical grounding, Coubertin's promotion of the amateur ideal became a pretext for making sure that poor, nonwhite, nonmale athletes need not apply to these new games. It was an agenda which found blunt expression from Caspar Whitney, of the American Olympic Committee, who referred to working-class athletes as "vermin."

With the foundation of the modern Olympics, which debuted in Athens in 1896, Coubertin and his colleagues, all of them rich, many possessing hereditary fortunes, were certain that they had created a movement that would ensure that the gentleman athlete could find an arena in which to compete untouched by the taint of professionalism. What they could never have suspected was that this supposedly apolitical festival would, in the coming century, become a forum for athletes of all races, sexes, and ethnicities, as well as the staging ground for some remarkably contentious political statements.

In fact, with the very first modern Olympic hero, the plan for a festival that was limited to an elite corps of aristocratic athletes was already under threat. On April 10, 1896, a small field of thirteen runners set out in the debut Olympic marathon, an event inspired by the story of Phidippides, that mythical runner of antiquity. Among the competitors was 23-year-old Spyridon Louis, a humble water carrier from Athens who, after stopping for a brandy along the route, entered the Olympic stadium in first place. The crowd, who had yet to see a Greek winner in track and field despite high early hopes, went wild. Louis was mobbed, most notably by two Greek princes. Later, he met with King George I himself, who offered Louis any prize he wanted. The exhausted winner could only think to ask for a donkey cart to carry the mineral water he sold, though later he would receive a variety of other prizes, including gold jewelry, from his ecstatic countrymen. A working-class runner receiving valuable rewards for his performance—Coubertin's amateur ideal had not even lasted for the duration of one Olympiad.

GIVEN the close cultural relationship of the United States and Great Britain, it was inevitable that the early American athlete appeared to follow a similar trajectory as his British counterpart. A period of savagery and rowdiness that lasted from the colonial era to the middle part of the 19th century gradually gave way to a more genteel atmosphere, in which amateurism and school-based games moved into the vanguard. Beneath the surface, however, by the 1870s the American athlete was already diverging from the British playbook, incorporating distinctly American ideals. Home-grown sports such as baseball, basketball, and football came to be seen as means of defining and expressing the evolving national character. Professional boxing and horse racing may have been denigrated by champions of British-style amateurism like Caspar Whitney, but they remained popular avenues for black and immigrant athletes, who knew they were not going to be invited into the gentlemen's locker room any time soon. Profit and victory may have been publicly frowned upon by the ruling classes, but anyone who understood the United States knew that it would not be long before these traits would start to exert considerable influence on the American athlete.

For all the power he now wields over the public's imagination and pocketbook, the American athlete had a very modest start. The press of Puritanism kept the nation virtually sports free for the first century after settlers arrived at Plymouth Rock. With the easing of puritanical influence as the 18th century progressed, athletic activities began to develop, albeit along strictly British lines. Horse racing was by far the most popular sport, drawing unprecedented crowds throughout the colonies. Bull-baiting, ratting, and cockfighting also became popular. These were inevitably accompanied by gambling. Pedestrianism and rowing also attracted large crowds, as did bare-knuckle fighting. In the South, boxers and other competitors were often slaves whose masters bet on their athletes like prize animals.

As in England, things began to change by the middle of the 19th century, a process that accelerated rapidly after the end of the Civil War. Amateurism became all the rage. The American

Athletic Union (AAU) was formed in 1888, its mission the strict enforcement of nonprofessional standards. Walter Camp, the Yale and Stanford football coach who was instrumental in inventing the game, claimed in 1893 that a "gentleman does not make his living . . . from his athletic prowess. He does not earn anything by his victories except glory and satisfaction." One can only wonder what he would have made of the $100 million deals made by the likes of the gentlemanly Peyton and Eli Manning a century later.

One of the hallmarks of the amateur athlete was a concept that had its origins in Britain but was taken up in America with special zeal—the muscular Christian. Its first champions were Charles Kingsley, a Church of England priest and author of the immensely popular 1855 novel *Westward Ho!*, and Thomas Hughes, author of the equally popular 1857 account of English public school life, *Tom Brown's School Days*. These men were able to perform some skillful mental gymnastics of their own by reconciling the tenets of Social Darwinism with those of Christ's Sermon on the Mount. For instance, Hughes famously claimed that "a man's body is given him to be trained and brought into subjection, and then used for the protection of the weak, the advancement of all righteous causes, and the subduing of the earth which God has given to the children of men."

Kingsley, whose robust Christianity did not inspire tolerance for the Irish, whom he called "white chimpanzees," found ready partners for his muscular Christianity in the United States, where clergymen such as Henry Ward Beecher and Thomas Wentworth Higginson took up the torch. They saw in athletics a means to create rugged, durable, virtuous Christians who would be able to carry the gospel aggressively into a hostile world. These ripped believers would also have a ready-made outlet for lustful impulses that might otherwise result in masturbation or fornication. Athletics became a cornerstone of religious education, leading to the spread of organizations like the Young Men's Christian Association (YMCA). One of Muscular Christianity's leading proponents was the legendary football coach Amos Alonzo Stagg, who in 1891 led the "Stubby Christians" team at the YMCA Training School in Springfield, Massachusetts. The following year, Stagg also played in the first public game of basketball, a sport invented by his colleague James Naismith as a way to occupy the energy of wayward boys.

As in England, this exemplary amateur found a home in the academy, primarily in the nation's colleges. The student-athlete, once nearly nonexistent in America, came to dominate its campuses. The first recorded interscholastic competition occurred in 1852, when Harvard and Yale rowed against each other on a New Hampshire lake. In 1869, the first college football game was played between Princeton and Rutgers. By the 1890s, very few colleges were immune from the epidemic. Not everyone was happy about this revolution. In a trend that would repeat itself over the next century, an active insurgency of professors and administrators began to push back against this emergent force on their campuses. In 1873, Cornell president Andrew White went so far as to cancel a game against Michigan, claiming: "I shall not permit 30 men to travel 400 miles merely to agitate a bag of wind."

But it was cynics like White who came to be seen as bags of wind. There was no stopping the athlete's ascent to the top of the college food chain. American "bloods" became the big men on campus. They differed, however, in one key respect from their British cousins. Simply "playing the game" was not enough. In the rapidly expanding United States, sports came to be seen as an end in itself rather than a means of acquiring the habits and values of good citizenry. Winning became paramount. The athlete was not someone who would bring the school glory by heroics performed later in life. He could bring it to the school immediately, through victory against rivals.

Despite the bromides of figures like Camp, coaches came to be seen as tacticians who could ensure these victories, rather than teachers whose job it was to mold future leaders. By the beginning of the 20th century, this thirst for victory at all costs had reached a fever pitch, especially in football, which now incorporated the savagery and competitive aggression that also characterized robber barons. Teams, like corporations, were expected to win at all costs. Increasingly often, that cost was human life. In the 1890s, a formation called the "flying wedge" was invented, in which a team would form an arrowhead of blockers who would bear down on any tackler who got in their way. Although technically banned soon afterward, it remained in widespread use through the turn of the century. Given the rudimentary nature of protective gear, the results were shocking in both the college and nascent professional ranks. In 1902, a dozen deaths on the playing field were recorded. Two years later, twenty were killed. Thirty died in 1909, including eight collegians. The carnage in college games was amplified by the recruitment of professionals, who were given incentives that would make even the most morally flexible contemporary recruiters blush. Most of the starters on the 1893 University of Michigan team were not students at all, but paid mercenaries. According to Robert Boyle in his fine study *Sport: Mirror of American Life*, "Yale lured

James Logan, a superb tackle, to New Haven at the turn of the century by giving him a suite at Vanderbilt Hall, free meals, a trip to Cuba, free tuition, a monopoly on the sale of scorecards, and a job as a cigarette agent for the American Tobacco Company." Muscles were no longer necessarily Christian. Victory culture reigned.

It was a crossroads for the athlete in America. Would the amateur survive, or would the athlete become thoroughly professionalized? The fray was joined by the era's premier sportsman, who also happened to be the nation's 26th president. Teddy Roosevelt was the Henry VIII of his times, a strapping, boisterous polymath who loved to hunt, hike, row, and box. Not surprisingly, this aristocratic scourge of monopolizing corporations came down decisively on the side of the amateur, threatening to ban football altogether unless the game cleaned up its act. His leadership led to the formation in 1910 of the National Collegiate Athletic Association (NCAA), whose explicit mission was "the regulation and supervision of college athletics throughout the United States in order that the athletic activities of the colleges and universities of the United States may be maintained on an ethical plane in keeping with the dignity and high purpose of education." As for the game of football itself, rules were changed to make it safer, most notably guidelines encouraging the forward pass.

Roosevelt's advocacy led directly to the most seminal, and perhaps the most exciting, moment in football history. It happened on November 1, 1913, during the first ever game between perennial powerhouses Army and Notre Dame. Few who watched the game would have known that Notre Dame, led by captain Knute Rockne, had been secretly practicing the forward pass during their preseason camp. Although legal for three years, the play was still largely reviled by traditionalists who saw it as a desecration of the game's rough-and-tumble essence. But Notre Dame knew that they would need it to beat their mighty opponents. Just as the game seemed to be settling into the usual slog of face-smashing running plays, Notre Dame quarterback Gus Dorais sent Rockne on a pattern that modern fans would recognize as a stop-and-go. The Army defender was caught flat-footed, and Rockne, who would go on to become college sport's most iconic coach, was able to haul in a 40-yard bomb for a touchdown. It must have looked as strange to the 5,000 astonished fans as the arrival of a flying saucer. "There had been no hurdling, no plunging, no crushing of fiber and sinew," Rockne would later proudly recall. "Just a long-distance touchdown plunge by rapid transit."

Roosevelt's thoughts on the role of the American athlete can best be seen in his famous speech "The American Boy," which memorably expresses the view of the amateur that had been developed on both sides of the Atlantic over the preceding seventy-five years. In it, he claims that sports have "an excellent effect in increased manliness," combating in particular the "effeminacy and luxury of young Americans who were born of rich parents." Right off the bat, TR betrays the era's belief that the ideal athlete was male, wealthy, and almost certainly, white. This potentially pampered schoolboy is able to prove himself "in manly exercises and to develop his body—and therefore, to a certain extent, his character—in the rough sports which call for pluck, endurance, and physical address." There is a danger, however, of overemphasizing victory, of seeing competition as a thing in itself. "When a man so far confuses ends and means as to think that fox-hunting, or polo, or foot-ball, or whatever else the sport may be, is to be itself taken as the end, instead of as the mere means of preparation to do work that counts when the time arises, when the occasion calls—why, that man had better abandon sport altogether." He ends the speech with an admonition that has made it a favorite of countless booster club dinners. "In short, in life, as in a foot-ball game, the principle to follow is: Hit the line hard; don't foul and don't shirk, but hit the line hard!"

TR's view found an unlikely echo in a speech given at Stanford University in 1906 by the pacifist psychologist William James. In it, he spoke of the need to find an enterprise that could serve as a substitute not just for battlefield slaughter, at which man was becoming increasingly efficient, but also to "the glory and shame that come to nations as well as to individuals from the ups and downs of politics and the vicissitudes of trade." James argued that as long as "antimilitarists propose no substitute for war's disciplinary function, no *moral equivalent* of war, analogous, as one might say, to the mechanical equivalent of heat, so long they fail to realize the full inwardness of the situation." Although he did not explicitly state that he saw sports as being this proxy, many have taken it for being just the thing, certainly more so than the rather fuzzy program of public works James suggested. In this view, training to become an athlete becomes a "stimulus . . . for awakening the higher ranges of men's spiritual energy." It is, quite simply, a means toward achieving the worthiest of goals—world peace.

In the end, these long-standing attempts to transform the athlete into the embodiment of man at his most vigorously civilized proved to be too great a weight for the icon to bear. World War I, with its unimaginable carnage, started less than a decade after James's speech. The following century saw geometric expansions in both humankind's ability to wage war and its passion for sports. The notion that athletic training would civilize humankind would have come as news to the victims at Passchendaele, Treblinka, and My Lai.

There were many in this era who could find little that was good to say about the growing worship of the athlete. Thorstein Veblen, one of America's most acute social critics, spoke with alarm about the "flesh worship" that lay at the heart of this revolution. In his *The Theory of the Leisure Class* (1899), Veblen argued that sports were simply another example of the affluent being able to wallow in the free time they had gained by exploiting the laboring class. It was a form of barbarism, a sign of man's attachment to his violent roots. "The addiction to sports, therefore, in a peculiar degree marks an arrested development in man's moral nature," he famously claimed in a chapter of the book titled "Modern Survivals of Prowess."

While Roosevelt and Veblen squabbled over the role of sports in a rapidly emerging society, the American athlete was in the process of inventing himself in the nation's meadows and on its city streets. Nowhere could this be seen more vividly than in the evolution of baseball, a sport that allowed the athlete to take on a peculiarly American accent. Its rules were established by New York's Knickerbocker Club in the 1840s. By 1858, there were 22 clubs in the National Association of Base Ball Players. The Civil War did nothing to stop the game's growth. In fact, the conflict helped it spread, with soldiers on both sides, from all over the warring nation, unified in a passion for the game. Four years after Appomattox, the Cincinnati Red Stockings became the first completely professional team. By the end of the century, baseball was the national pastime.

The athletes who played the game expressed the national character. Baseball's similarities to workplace and domestic life were striking. Although individual acts of excellence and courage were rewarded, it ultimately encouraged conformity. Victory required teamwork, with groups of men from varying backgrounds and ethnicities (though rarely blacks) joining together in a common task under the supervision of a boss, the coach. With the introduction in 1879 of a reserve clause that bound players to their team, the athlete became an employee working for a company. Scientific rationalization was applied—games were governed by an elaborate set of rules; statistics became increasingly important. Games ended when the task at hand had been completed. Employees were expected to work overtime if the game went into extra innings. At the end of a successful offensive play, the athlete found himself returning "home." Sports may or may not have formed an individual's character, as Roosevelt desired and Veblen feared; there could be little doubt that, in the case of baseball, the athlete was formed *by* the nation's character.

Any chance that the game would not become purely red, white, and blue was laid to rest during Roosevelt's presidency, when sports equipment magnate Albert Goodwill Spalding launched an "investigation" to establish that the game's origins were strictly American, and not based on the British game of rounders, as the English-born journalist (and inventor of the box score) Henry Chadwick maintained. The widely heralded (and, to this day, still credulously accepted) results of this sporting Warren Commission solemnly announced that baseball was invented in 1839 by Abner Doubleday in Cooperstown, New York. Although you could steal second, third, and home through the gaping holes in the Spalding report, nobody was much interested in questioning it. The myth served. America had its sport—and its first all-star team of iconic athletes. Early superstars like Christy Mathewson, nicknamed "The Christian Gentleman," and Honus "The Flying Dutchman" Wagner were cut from the same cloth as the fans who watched them. These were neither paid outlaws nor haughty amateurs, but regular guys with specialized skills who were out to put in a solid day's work. Even a problematical character like Ty Cobb, known for his dirty play, could be easily assimilated once he was understood as being like the local bully or factory-floor crank. The athlete had become someone fans could see as one of their own. They could relate to him. The game he played was familiar, something many in the stands had played themselves as boys. The athlete had become the spawn of the turbulent, evolving river of everyday American life.

It was a process greatly aided by the dizzying advances in the nation's communications and transportation infrastructures. Athletes could travel from city to city with growing ease; their stories and images proliferated in an increasing number of newspapers and magazines. By the time of America's entry into World War I, Americans were bombarded with information about not just baseball stars, but a wide variety of sportsmen. Familiarity bred affection, not contempt. The athlete was becoming ingrained in America's daily life. And America had replaced England as his main arena. The stage was set for his apotheosis to a central position in his culture's imagination. He was about to become a hero.

CHAPTER 6

THE FAITH OF 50 MILLION

The years directly following World War I were a critical time for the athlete. The grinding slaughter in the trenches had devastated a generation. Ten million young men had died in battle. Given this legacy, few were eager to celebrate the warrior-like qualities of the athlete. From the British public schools and the Ivy League to the workingmen's clubs of Yorkshire and boxing gyms of Hell's Kitchen, the idea that robust games prepared young men for righteous battle must have seemed risible. Everyone knew what machine guns and mustard gas could do to healthy bodies. Roosevelt's admonition to "hit the line hard!" took on a grim new meaning in the wake of infantry charges that had resulted in thousands of casualties in a matter of minutes.

What must have seemed especially grotesque were the attempts in the early days of the war to use the athlete's paraphernalia as a way of inspiring heroism among the troops. Stories of soldiers going "over the top" as they wielded cricket bats or kicked soccer balls were recognized as the acts of madmen. The most famous of these sporting charges occurred in 1915, at the Battle of Loos. As the British were preparing to advance on the German lines, soldiers of the London Irish Rifles regiment came up with the idea of dribbling a half dozen soccer balls among themselves as they headed across no-man's-land toward the "goal" of the German trenches. Officers discovered the scheme before it could be enacted and ordered the balls destroyed. One of them, however, was sneaked into battle. Advancing soldiers were able to boot it several times before the sergeant playing center forward was cut down. The ball got caught up in barbed wire, though it was subsequently retrieved and can currently be seen in the regimental museum in London. Anyone tempted to view this incident as an example of the sort of "pluck" that Roosevelt believed sports could inspire should bear in mind that 75,000 soldiers were killed or wounded in that battle, which resulted in only minimal Allied gains. Loos was also the first time that the British deployed poison gas during World War I. A more humane use of the athlete during the war can be found in the stories of soccer being played between groups of enemy soldiers during lulls in the fighting, such as happened during the spontaneous Christmas truce of 1914. It is unlikely anyone cared too much about the score during these "friendlies." The never-ending tally of the dead would have provided all the results anyone might want.

If there ever was a time when athletes were needed to rescue the public from grim reality, it was during those early postwar years. In America, however, the first truly headline-grabbing sports story was anything but heroic. The Black Sox scandal, which broke in the autumn of 1920, seemed specially designed to confirm the cynicism that had been born on the fields of Flanders. It began when eight members of the Chicago White Sox, considered the best team in baseball, were accused of throwing the 1919 World Series, the first played since the Armistice. The players, many of whom considered themselves grossly underpaid, agreed to lose in exchange for $100,000 in payments from a gambling syndicate led by the notorious New York mobster Arnold Rothstein. All eight players earned lifetime suspensions. The most notable among them was the great left fielder "Shoeless" Joe Jackson. Although he originally confessed to taking a $5,000 bribe, Jackson later recanted and went to his grave maintaining his innocence, submitting as evidence the fact that he played productively throughout the series, which Cincinnati won 5 to 3 (the Series was best of 9 games back then).

Despite this blow, people continued to believe. Not even a scandal this profound could diminish their allegiance to the athlete. Just as modern player strikes (or management lockouts, depending on your viewpoint) never seem to result in the predicted exodus of fans in our times, so this clear-cut betrayal of public faith could not dissuade increasing numbers of people in that era from forking over their hard-earned money to watch the athlete perform in a series of glorious new stadiums and arenas.

The 1920s are known as the golden age of sports in the United States. The athlete had never been more powerful or influential. A booming economy and an increasingly sophisticated transportation network made the athlete ever more accessible to the public. Every season seemed to produce a new crop of heroes. This explosion was greatly aided by a rapidly expanding mass media. Although sportswriters had been hyperactive in the United States since the 1830s, it was during the 1920s that they came into their own, often transforming sports pages into the most popular sections of a newspaper. Writers like Damon Runyon, Paul Gallico, and Grantland Rice became stars in their own right. Although their writing styles varied, all of them were acutely aware of what their readers wanted. Heroes. In his coverage of the Notre Dame football team's upset win over Army in 1924, Rice was simply giving the public what it wanted when he produced the golden era's richest nugget of prose.

> Outlined against a blue-gray October sky, the Four Horsemen rode again. In dramatic lore their names are Death, Destruction, Pestilence, and Famine. But those are aliases. Their real names are: Stuhldreher, Crowley, Miller and Layden. They formed the crest of the South Bend cyclone before which another fighting Army team was swept over the precipice at the Polo Grounds this afternoon as 55,000 spectators peered down upon the bewildering panorama spread out upon the green plain below.

Clearly, this was a man who understood he was in the legend-making business. Rice would later famously quip that "when a sportswriter stops making heroes out of athletes, it's time to get out of the business." As hagiographers, these sportswriters also understood something that would seem anathema to their successors. They truly believed that they had no business exposing many of the sins they discovered through their proximity to their subjects. Rice and his colleagues often found themselves playing a tricky double game, providing their increasingly broad audiences with supposedly intimate portraits of athletes even as they held back information about substance abuse, sexual deviancy, or outright criminality, the sort of dirt that fans would expect to be served up as a matter of course a half century later.

This doublethink could be seen most vividly in the coverage of the era's most iconic athlete, Babe Ruth. Although the Yankee slugger's on-field accomplishments were prodigious, especially for those pre-steroidal times, his fame was greatly aided by the breathlessly reverential treatment he received from the press. With his pudgy frame, lovably ugly mug, and winning smile, Ruth was portrayed as an overgrown pajama-clad boy who had emerged from a Baltimore boy's home to play the game with an exuberance that spilled over into his private life. His worst excesses were cast as harmless japery. Rumors may have occasionally leaked out, especially when he nearly died of an unspecified stomach ailment during spring training in 1925, but the prodigious sexual encounters, the gambling debts, and the binge drinking remained known only to a closely knit circle of friends and teammates, as well as to a pack of reliably discreet journalists whose obligation was to sell papers, not tell the truth.

Burnished by an adoring press, Ruth's public image glowed more brilliantly than anyone who came before him, and arguably since. Although he would have probably made the Hall of Fame if he had remained a dazzling left-handed pitcher for the Boston Red Sox, it was with his move to the Yankees in 1920 that he achieved iconic status. Playing in the media capital of the nation contributed greatly to Ruth's popularity, though it was his switch from pitcher to hitter that proved even more decisive. Of course, there were other great batters in the game at the time, such as Ty Cobb and Rogers Hornsby. It was Ruth's ability to master that most quintessential of American athletic feats, the home run, that earned him unparalleled fame. Before him, the home run had been a relatively rare phenomenon. In 1917, Wally Pipp led the American League in home runs with nine, improving on Braggo Roth's 1915 total of seven. Part of this scarcity had to do with a "dead ball"—cork-centered baseballs were not introduced until 1910, and rumors still persist that the current "live" ball was not in full use until 1919. Also, the game's leading strategists, namely the great New York Giants manager John McGraw, simply did not believe in the home run. They thought is was a waste of energy to swing for the fences. Instead, they championed "inside baseball," a game in which bunts, stolen bases, and the hit-and-run were used to eke out one run at a time.

Ruth changed all of this. He swung mightily, amassing jaw-dropping numbers in the process. In 1920, his first year as a Yankee, he hit 54 home runs. The following year, he hit 59. The runners-up in the American League during those years hit 19 and 24. And Ruth was not afraid to strike out trying. On some misses, his body would corkscrew around completely, even sending him sprawling into the dirt beside home plate. "I swing big, with everything I've got," he explained. "I hit big or miss. I like to live as big as I can."

It was a style that proved a perfect fit for the boom time of the Roaring Twenties. The entire nation was swinging for the fences, from Wall Street to Hollywood. It was inevitable that its signature hero would do the same. Ruth quickly became an iconic presence throughout the culture, barnstorming to small towns to play in front of people who could not afford to travel to the big cities, mugging for photographs in bizarre costumes, appearing in a string of cheaply made but popular short films. Fellow players were bemused by the vast amount of time Ruth spent signing autographs for his adoring public, especially children. While part of this might have been due to his lingering recollection of his own hardscrabble youth, it also reflected his instinctual appreciation for his place at the epicenter of the American imagination.

Myths grew around him like a Homeric hero. Their sketchy provenance did nothing to diminish their power. In one, he allegedly promised an 11-year-old boy named Johnny Sylvester, gravely ill in the hospital, that he would hit a home run for him that day—which he proceeded to do. Perhaps the most famous Babe-myth involved the "called shot" during the 1932 World Series, when, in the course of a contentious third game against the Chicago Cubs at Wrigley Field, Ruth supposedly pointed to a spot deep in the center field bleachers, where he then parked the next pitch. While there is no conclusive evidence he actually pointed to the bleachers, there can be no doubt that it was the sort of thing fans expected him to do.

The decade's other signature athlete was Jack Dempsey, the heavyweight champion of the world from 1919 until 1926. Not particularly big or skilled at the finer points of the "sweet science," Dempsey won by unleashing savage assaults on his opponents. Dempsey benefited from being the first champion to fight in an era when boxing had largely been legalized, and his popularity came close to matching Ruth's. His 1921 title defense against Georges Carpentier was both the first to be broadcast by radio and the first $1 million gate in boxing history. Five years later, 120,000 people turned out to watch his title fight in Philadelphia against Gene Tunney, which doubled the gate of the Carpentier match.

What makes Dempsey so representative of his era was the ease with which he translated his athletic success into fame. With a movie star's practiced charm, he completed his sport's migration from swampy secret venues and offshore sites into the glare of mega-stadiums. Before he became famous, John L. Sullivan fought hundreds of fights, and probably made even more appearances on the theatrical stage, often just standing shirtless before small crowds of gaping yokels. Mass media made things much easier for Dempsey. Although he had been raised dirt-poor in Colorado, and even lived as a hobo for a while in his teens, Dempsey was blessed with an appreciation for the mechanics of publicity. He understood the fundamentals of supply and demand in a roaring economy. Over the seven-year period he was champ, he defended his title only six times, greatly increasing the gate while also maintaining his looks and health for out-of-the-ring activities. Like Ruth, he made himself part of the nation's daily vernacular. While champion, he appeared in movies, married a Hollywood actress, and endorsed a variety of products. Guided by the cunning promoter Tex Rickard, Dempsey also cultivated relationships with sportswriters, providing them with fodder for their ever-expanding pages. They showed their appreciation by treating him like a god.

It was not just big-name stars who fed this brave new publicity machine. In the 1920s, American life became thoroughly athleticized. People were mad for the athlete. Popular culture became laden with songs, films, and advertisements about sports heroes. The nation's rapidly expanding advertising industry began to use athletes as engines to move merchandise. Ruth and Notre Dame coach Knute Rockne rented their clean-shaven jowls to Barbasol to sell its shaving cream; football star Red Grange sold Coca-Cola. Wheaties cereal, "The Breakfast of Champions," was introduced in 1924; endorsements from athletes like Lou Gehrig were appearing regularly by the early 1930s, starting a tradition that continues today with LeBron James. In *The Freshman* (1925), whose climactic sequence was shot at an actual UC Berkeley–Stanford game, Harold Lloyd attempted to gain popularity at his college with a novel method—he joined the football team.

There seemed to be no end to the demand for images of competition and sporting spectacle. Everybody wanted to be an athlete. Feats of endurance were all the rage. If people could not play baseball or football or golf or tennis, they would invent a sport. Flagpole sitting became popular, with characters such as Shipwreck Kelly spending weeks at a time balanced atop poles. Dance marathons could drag on for days; Charleston contests produced stars like Ginger Rogers, Joan Crawford, and Carole Lombard. When American Gertrude Ederle became the first woman to swim the English Channel in 1926, she returned home to a ticker-tape parade, a movie deal, and a meeting with President Coolidge. Her reception proved little more than a dress rehearsal for that awaiting Charles Lindbergh, that unrivaled athlete of the air, the following year.

No contemporary work of art illuminates the omnipresence of the athlete better than F. Scott Fitzgerald's *The Great Gatsby*, published in 1925. Unlike Rice, however, the novelist was willing to show that the American athlete could often be a deeply corrupt figure. It often feels as if Fitzgerald spent as much time at Princeton reading Veblen as he did watching the Tigers play. Daisy Buchanan's languid friend Jordan Baker, who oozes ennui and cynicism, is a women's golfing champion whose "pleasing contemptuous expression" could be seen in "many rotogravure pictures of the sporting life at Asheville and Hot Springs and Palm Beach." Gatsby's associate Meyer Wolfsheim, based on

Arnold Rothstein, is breezily introduced by Gatsby to the novel's narrator, Nick Carraway, as "the man who fixed the World's Series back in 1919." Carraway is aghast that a single man could be responsible for playing with "the faith of 50 million people." And then there is Daisy's abusive, racist husband Tom, who still possesses the "cruel body" he forged when he was "one of the most powerful ends that ever played football at New Haven—a national figure in a way, one of those men who reach such an acute limited excellence at twenty-one that everything afterward savors of anticlimax." At a time when the athlete was seen as a hero, Fitzgerald suggested that this obsession with competition and physical performance had a darker side. Those 50 million people, whom Rice and his colleagues cast as the blessed faithful, could actually be a very large bunch of suckers.

In Europe, the postwar athlete was forced into a similarly redemptive role as in the States, though with considerably less hype. Where young men had been expending their energy pulverizing one another just a few years earlier, during the twenties they were urged to use their power and skill to stitch together the shattered continent. Much weight was placed on the Olympics, which briefly did manage to achieve Coubertin's dream of serving as a festival of brotherhood. The victories of British sprinters Harold Abrahams and Eric Liddell in the 1924 Paris Games, immortalized in the Oscar-winning film *Chariots of Fire*, were seen as triumphs of amateurism and quiet resolve, as were the astonishing accomplishments of the Finnish distance runner Paavo Nurmi, who won five gold medals at the same games, including two (in the 1500 and 5000 meters) within less than an hour of each other. In the professional ranks, meanwhile, soccer continued its relentless ascent as the sport of the masses, not just in England but on the European continent, where players in Spain, Italy, France, and just about every other country provided the laboring classes with a series of heroes they could claim for themselves.

In Germany, the athlete was co-opted as an icon by two diametrically opposed forces within the traumatized nation. The glittering but shaky Weimar Republic went through a "boximania" not unlike that experienced in Regency England. As is so often the case with European appropriation of American popular culture, many Germans in the 1920s overreached. They regarded boxing as it was currently being practiced in the slums of New York and Chicago as a sort of high art that profoundly expressed the modern condition. As Kasia Boddy points out, "if Americans indulged in the trivialities of popular culture as a way of shrugging off serious matters, Germans took it all very seriously. To champion American movies and sports stars was a way for many to assert their allegiance to modernity and to reject the nostalgic mode of much German culture." The European (and eventual world) heavyweight champion Max Schmeling became a particular favorite of Berlin's cabarets and salons, his image memorably captured by the artist George Grosz in 1926.

Another painter, this one not nearly as successful or talented as Grosz, also had his eye on the boxer as a symbol of a new Germany. Although Adolf Hitler disparaged most organized sports as decadent and Jewish-controlled, he did manage to see the political value of boxing. "There is no sport that cultivates a spirit of aggressiveness, that develops the body to such steely smoothness," he gushed in *Mein Kampf*, sounding more like a budding sportswriter than a dictator in the making.

AND then came the Great Depression. The boom time was over. The hitting streak turned into a long slump. At first, the decline did little to dampen the public's enthusiasm for the athlete, even as some of them were getting hit hard, most notably Jack Dempsey, who reportedly lost $3 million in the crash. When asked in 1930 how he could justify making more money than President Hoover, Babe Ruth allegedly answered, "Why not? I had a better year than he did." In fact, even the Bambino would soon be taking a pay cut. Although baseball attendance actually rose in the year after the great crash, as the decade wore on and the magnitude of the Depression sank in, people stopped coming out to the ball game in the great numbers they had during the recent boom years. Even Connie Mack's legendary Philadelphia Athletics, who had won the World Series in 1929 and 1930, were eventually broken up after the flamboyant owner/manager was forced to sell off several of his best players.

Among the stars Mack was forced to flog was the slugger Jimmie Foxx, one of the greatest power hitters in the history of the game. Many who watched him compared his batting to Ruth's. The differences between the two men's images could not, however, have been greater. The icon was losing its golden veneer. Where Ruth, whose litany of nicknames included "The Caliph of Clout" and "The Sultan of Swat," possessed a gilded persona that perfectly encapsulated his era, Foxx's public image was very much in tune with his more hard-bitten times. Known as "The Beast," his one showy gesture was to cut off the sleeves of his jersey so opposing pitchers would see his arm muscles ripple as he prepared to swing. Other than that, he was all business as he went about driving tape measure home runs into bleachers occupied by dwindling crowds of men who had a one-in-four chance of being unemployed. Off the field, Foxx's life mirrored those of many in the stands. There were few celebrity appearances. No one asked him to mug for the camera. A sullen drinker, he lost most of his wages on a series of ill-advised investments. After kicking around in a number of make-work jobs in baseball after retirement, he died at the age of 59 by choking on a piece of meat.

The decade's best player was Lou Gehrig of the New York Yankees, who also turned out to be perhaps the signature athletic icon of the Depression era. Born to poor German immigrants in New York City, he briefly attended Columbia University before joining the New York Yankees, for whom he played from 1923 to 1939. Although his batting statistics are among the greatest in baseball history, he will always be best remembered for playing in 2,130 consecutive games, a record which held until it was finally broken by Cal Ripken Jr. in 1995. It was later discovered that Gehrig suffered 17 fractures in his hands during the streak, which ended in 1939 only after he was stricken with ALS (amyotrophic lateral sclerosis), which of course came to be known afterward as Lou Gehrig's disease.

It was the sportswriter Paul Gallico, one of the foremost star makers of the golden age, who suggested that the Yankees stage a Lou Gehrig Appreciation Day on the 4th of July of that same year. Gehrig's faltering appearance on the playing field led to one of the most iconic moments in the history of the athlete, as his echoing voice assured a packed Yankee Stadium that, even though he had been given a "bad break," he considered himself "the luckiest man on the face of the earth." The initial reaction of most fans sitting in the stadium or listening on radios at home might well have been that nothing could be further from the truth. Even those who did not grasp the devastating severity of ALS could nonetheless sense that it must be a fearsome disease indeed that could transform this 36-year-old man from one of the toughest athletes in history into such a stricken figure. And yet many of those same fans, who had just endured a decade of hardship themselves, would also come to understand that the unassuming man they were watching, who had showed up every day for a job he never lost and always loved, was in fact very lucky. He had occupied that enchanted space most people spent so much time only dreaming about inhabiting, the diamond at Yankee Stadium. And he had done it quietly, steadily, modestly, even as more charismatic stars like Babe Ruth and Joe DiMaggio shone beside him. Although athletes are almost always young men and women who simply want to compete and win, occasionally what they do on the field of play allows them to capture the essence of their times. Ruth and Dempsey had managed to do this in the 1920s; Muhammad Ali and Michael Jordan would do the same for their eras. Depression-era America, where simple endurance had become the core virtue of the common man, belonged to Lou Gehrig like no other athlete.

There were many other athletes who filled the need for working-class heroes. When they did, their achievements were often trumpeted by sportswriters who understood the changing tastes of their readers. The boxer James Braddock may not have been the most gifted heavyweight champion of the era, but he was the one who most powerfully fired the imaginations of the American public. After a promising start to his boxing career, the former dockworker badly injured his right hand. The fights stopped coming in the early 1930s. His family fell on hard times, and Braddock was forced to return to work on the docks. To his lasting shame, he was also forced to accept charity. He was finally able to return to the ring in 1934, though only as a stepping-stone for younger fighters. He shocked everyone by winning bouts, and within a year had defeated Max Baer in a stunning upset for the heavyweight championship. The sportswriter Damon Runyon tirelessly hyped Braddock's story, a myth-making process capped when Runyon nicknamed Braddock the "The Cinderella Man." As had happened with Gehrig, personal hardship and gritty forbearance were replacing jazzy charisma as the athlete's favored personality. Sportswriters were learning just how malleable this action figure could be.

In England, hard times also defined the athlete, especially those who played the signature sport of the working classes. Despite unemployment rates that were at times even higher than those in the United States, soccer remained remarkably popular, the terraces of stadiums filling on Saturdays with men who could feel kinship with players whose salaries were capped at just a few pounds per week. The era's foremost player, Stanley Matthews of Stoke City, was in many ways the British equivalent of Lou Gehrig, at least before the baseball player fell ill. The son of a barber, Matthews was capable of explosive moments of ball-handling wizardry. He was also considered the consummate gentleman. But good manners only go so far, especially when an athlete is compelled to labor year after year for a perennial also-ran like Stoke. In 1937, Matthews suggested he wanted to transfer to a team that actually had a chance of winning the championship. A thousand placard-wielding fans gathered outside Stoke's stadium to protest the move. They might have lost their jobs, but they were not about to lose their star. Matthews quietly agreed to stay and would remain at Stoke for another decade. You could not be a working-class hero if you started acting like a boss. The world was not yet ready for the free agent.

IN addition to serving as a model for proletarian endurance, the athlete also became a focus for the political turbulence that marked the decade running up to World War II. Politicians of all ideologies came to understand the athlete's importance as a propaganda instrument. His contests often became shorthand for international conflicts and cultural shifts.

The infamous "bodyline" cricket incident between England and Australia was an example of sports being used to act out deeper tensions. In the autumn of 1932, the English national cricket team began a tour of Australia as part of the ongoing Ashes series between the two countries. The Australians had won the previous meeting in 1930 due to the epic batting of Don Bradman, generally considered the greatest player in the history of the sport. In order to stop his expected onslaught this time around, the English captain, Douglas Jardine, devised a technique called bodyline, in which the ball would be bowled directly at the batter's body in an effort to intimidate him into playing easily catchable shots.

To anyone raised on brushback pitches in baseball, this would seem to be a fairly standard tactical adjustment to deal with a man who was expected to single-handedly win the Ashes cup, the most important totem in the rivalry between England and her former colony. After all, there was nothing illegal about bodyline bowling. Nevertheless, Jardine's decision became a major scandal. The Australians believed that the English captain, a snob and xenophobe who did little to hide his venomously condescending attitude toward Australians, was deliberately trying to injure the opposing batters. Jardine and the English press reacted to these protests with withering contempt, suggesting that the Australians were simply being "squealers."

English condescension hit a raw nerve among the Australians, reminding them of their history as a dumping ground for British convicts as well as the fact that this former colony was still culturally and economically dependent on its ex-rulers. The situation deteriorated even further when the Australian captain famously told England's general manager after one particularly heated day's play that "there are two teams out there. One is playing cricket; the other is not." The Australian cricket board then sent a cable to their counterparts in London calling the English tactics "unsportsmanlike." This proved to be a grave libel to the English, whose entire athletic cosmos was based upon the notion of fair play, whether they were actually practicing it or not. They demanded an apology and threatened grave consequences if none were forthcoming. Faced with prospect of a boycott by their major trading partner, the Aussies were forced to back down. England won the series 4 to 1, though the notion that they were exemplars of fair play became a more difficult proposition to maintain, especially Down Under.

Such political conflicts played themselves out in stadiums throughout the 1930s. The athlete became a pawn in a wide variety of conflicts. During the Spanish Civil War, the famous rivalry between the Barcelona and Real Madrid soccer clubs took on dark overtones when the latter squad came to be seen as the home team of the fascist leader Francisco Franco's faction. Their rivals from Barcelona served as models of not only Catalan nationalism but also the entire Republican movement. "Barca's" stadium was one of the few places where people felt free to speak the Catalan language after it was banned by the nationalists. Sporting enmity between the two sides reached a deadly intensity in 1936, when fascist thugs kidnapped and murdered Barcelona's team president, Josep Sunyol i Garriga. To this day, the yearly games between the two clubs, known as El Clásico, take on an intensity and political importance that transcends soccer, a fact reflected in FC Barcelona's motto, *més que un club*—more than just a club.

Soccer also became a forum for fascist politics during the 1934 World Cup, hosted by Mussolini's Italy. In what can now be seen as a sort of dry run for Hitler's Olympics two years later, Il Duce used the tournament as a means of promoting the strength and efficiency of his ideology. The dictator himself became a preening, saluting presence in the crowd at the host team's games. Anyone doubting his desire to politicize the tournament need only look at the name of the venue in Rome where the championship game was held—The Stadium of the National Fascist Party. The Italians won that game against Czechoslovakia 2 to 1, though their 4-to-2 victory over Hungary in the final in France four years later must have been even sweeter for the players. Just before that game, Mussolini sent his team a telegram that read *Vincere o morire*—"Win or Die." Although this exhortation is rather common in Italy and may not have been intended literally, any time a murderous psychopath who also happens to control your nation uses the phrase "or die" in a command, it is probably wise to take it seriously. Upon hearing of Mussolini's telegram after the game, Hungarian goalkeeper Antal Szabó quipped, "I may have let in four goals, but at least I saved their lives."

This politicization of the athlete in the 1930s reached its greatest intensity in two famous showdowns, both of which pitted Americans against Germans. The fact that both of the Americans were black, and were not considered equals by many of their own countryman, did little to diminish the iconic magnitude of these events. The fight between Joe Louis and Max Schmeling will be discussed in the next chapter in terms of its significance for the athlete as a racial figure, though let it suffice for now to say that in 1938 the symbolism of a German and an American slugging it out was lost on very few spectators on either side of the Atlantic. As with the players in the Barcelona–Real Madrid matches, the boxers were transformed into toy soldiers onto whom fans could project their hopes and fears.

While Jesse Owens's triumph in the Berlin Olympics in front of an unsmiling Hitler had profound racial implications back in the United States, the sprinter's four gold medals also undermined the dictator's political agenda. The Nazi Olympics, as the 1936 games came to be called, was one of the clearest examples in history of a regime attempting to use the athlete to support a political ideology. As previously mentioned, Hitler was not the most promising candidate to elevate his country's athletes to iconic status. He believed that sports, especially those that relied upon individual performance, squandered civic energy that could be better spent training the army, staging vast political rallies, or persecuting Jews. But he was also a supreme opportunist. Urged on by his propaganda minister Joseph Goebbels, Hitler not only threw his backing behind the German heavyweight boxing champion Schmeling but also provided full support to the 1936 Berlin Olympics. The Third Reich's chief architect, Albert Speer, was drafted to help give the Olympic stadium sufficiently monumental dimensions, while the brilliant filmmaker Leni Riefenstahl, fresh from her 1935 propaganda masterpiece *Triumph of the Will*, was tasked with capturing the games on film. Special training facilities were established for athletes. Gypsies were rounded up, though the brutal suppression of Jews eased temporarily to mollify foreign critics. The game's organizers even dreamed up an authentic-looking "ancient" torch relay that in fact never happened at the original Greek games.

Hitler's plans for a racial set piece were almost ruined when American Jews and other activists tried to organize a boycott of the games to protest not only Germany's general atmosphere of anti-Semitism but also specific laws that banned German Jews from participating in sports, in direct violation of the Olympic credo. The amateur middleweight champion Daniel Seelig had been kicked out of the German Boxing Association in 1933 for being a Jew, while the tennis star Daniel Prenn, one of the world's top-ranked players, was essentially banned from the sport after the German Tennis Federation passed a rule stating that "no Jew may be selected for a national team or the Davis Cup."

The most controversial victim of this anti-Semitism was the world champion fencer Helene Mayer. While studying in California in 1933, she was informed that, due to her having a Jewish father, she would no longer be eligible to compete for her native country. Her situation changed when protests finally caused the American

Athletic Union to vote to boycott the Berlin Games. Although their vote was not binding on US Olympians, Hitler and Goebbels feared that the tide was turning against them. Understanding the damage an American boycott would cause their showpiece, they instructed that Mayer be offered a place on the German team. The fact that she was tall, blonde, and photogenic no doubt made their decision easier to swallow. Despite pressure from American protesters, Mayer agreed to compete for her native country, explaining that she feared for the safety of her mother and two brothers, who still lived in Germany. Many accepted this rationale, though her peers would find it harder to absolve her for giving a Nazi salute on the victory podium after she won the silver medal.

In the end, Hitler probably need not have bothered letting Mayer fence. Despite some early success, the movement behind a boycott was faced with an immovable object if it was to keep the United States out of Berlin—Avery Brundage, the president of the American Olympic Committee. After being taken on a carefully scripted tour of Germany by Nazi officials in 1934, Brundage proclaimed that concerns about the Third Reich's racial policies were baseless. When protests continued, he wrote a pamphlet titled *Fair Play for American Athletes*, in which he characterized the boycott as a "Jewish-Communist conspiracy." In one of the most egregious examples of false equivalency on record, he also warned that athletes should not get dragged into "the present Jew-Nazi altercation." Brundage would go on to serve as president of the International Olympic Committee from 1952 to 1972.

The boycott averted, all that was now left for Hitler's athletes to do was to win. And that is precisely what the Germans did, easily beating America by winning 89 medals, 33 of which were gold.

The haul was enough to inspire Hitler to order Speer to start planning a 400,000-seat Olympic stadium, where the games would be held every four years once the world came under Nazi rule.

There were, however, four gold medals the Germans famously did *not* win, in the 100- and 200-meter sprints, the long jump, and the 4 x 100-meter relay. While Jesse Owens is often credited with spoiling Hitler's games, it is probable that the sprinter did not spend much time thinking about the man with the funny moustache at all. Like almost all great athletes, the 22-year-old Alabama native, fresh from a record-breaking career at Ohio State University, almost certainly focused exclusively on the task at hand, the fleeting moment when his long training would be put to the test for a few seconds of supreme competition. Riefenstahl's footage of Owens competing brings home just how self-contained an athlete he was, not only in his marvelously compact running style but also in the polite intensity with which he carried himself around the Olympic stadium. (Owens would famously decline to speak ill of the dictator, saying it was in "bad taste to criticize the man of the hour in another country.") Hitler's refusal to shake Owens's hand may or may not have stemmed from racist peevishness—it is possible that the Führer, never one for pressing the flesh anyway, had simply decided to stop shaking all foreign hands at that point. Whatever the reason, it seems likely that Owens could not have cared less. He was simply a young athlete taking quiet delight in his extraordinary abilities. Similarly, his famous friendship with the German long jumper Luz Long was probably not intended as a political statement, but rather stemmed from the sort of sudden bond that springs up among rival athletes in the heat of competition, especially when they know they are pushing one another to peak performances. By failing to acknowledge the propaganda and controversy swirling around him, Owens may have made the deepest, most enduring political statement possible.

THREE summers later, Hitler was to have his war. Athletes were once again folded into military ranks. Although baseball continued to be played, many of its greatest stars became part of the war effort, including Joe DiMaggio, who just months before the attack on Pearl Harbor had set a 56-game hitting streak that many consider the greatest individual achievement by any American athlete. Ted Williams, who had batted .406 the same season as DiMaggio's record, served as a Marine aviator, though not until after an ugly fight with the government in which he tried to have his draft status lowered. The dispute cost Williams some of his more patriotic fans, as well as his sponsorship deal with Quaker Oats, suggesting that the cereal's adherence to pacifism was only box deep.

While many of the top American and British athletes who entered the armed forces never saw frontline duty, some from other countries were less fortunate. Luz Long was killed during the fighting in Sicily in 1943, while Janusz Kusociński, who won the 10,000-meter gold medal in the 1932 Olympic Games, was executed by the Gestapo for serving in the Polish resistance. The most astonishing story of athletes during the war came from the Dynamo Kiev soccer team in 1942. After the Ukrainian capital fell, members of this famous squad were given jobs in a local bakery. The Germans discovered the players and decided to reconstitute the team so that it could provide "friendly" competition for German sides. The real plan, of course, was to create a forum in which Germans could demonstrate their national and racial superiority by whipping the Slavs. Dynamo had other plans. After they took the lead in their first game, they were threatened with execution unless they let the Germans win. Undeterred, the players went on to score a decisive victory. After two more defeats, the increasingly agitated Nazis shipped in an undefeated professional team from the fatherland. They, too, lost to the Ukrainians. Playing in an atmosphere of increasing menace that included occasional warning shots fired by SS officers in the stands, the home team was given one more chance to lose when they played yet another German professional team. Dynamo won 8 to 0. The team was quickly disbanded and, according to legend, its players arrested. Some were tortured and executed, others died in labor camps.

The decade following World War II saw a series of remarkable performances by athletes, from Bobby Thomson hitting the "shot heard 'round the world" home run to win the 1951 National League pennant to Roger Bannister breaking the 4-minute mile on an Oxford track in 1954. Even Sir Edmund Hillary's and Tenzing Norgay's 1953 ascent of Mount Everest can be seen as an unprecedented athletic achievement. The proliferation of network television made the athlete an increasingly accessible figure, especially in the United States, where baseball, football, and boxing began to fill up the endless succession of broadcast hours.

For all his excellence and visibility, there seemed to be something missing from the postwar athlete. After the intense iconic workout he had been given during the Roaring Twenties, the Great Depression, and World War II, he seemed to have exhausted much of his ability to serve as a symbol for the culture's deeper currents. Or perhaps he *did* symbolize something—the era's overwhelming conformity. He had become bland, almost two-dimensional, the sporting equivalent of the Man in the Gray Flannel Suit. Suddenly, those impassive faces of figures like baseball's Stan Musial, basketball's Bob Cousy, and boxing's Rocky Marciano did not stand for anything except an ability to play the game as well as anyone ever had.

The athlete's insularity during this era received memorable treatment in Frederick Exley's classic novel *A Fan's Notes*, published in 1968 but set in the previous decade. The book's narrator, also named Frederick Exley, is an alcoholic would-be writer who develops an infatuation with Frank Gifford, the star of the New York Giants football team. Fred, as he is known, first encounters Gifford when both attend the University of Southern California in the early 1950s. "Giff" is the Big Man on Campus, an All-American whose status is like "the Pope in the Vatican" or the screen idol Tony Curtis. He is aloof, resplendent, and perfect. Fred, a sneering English major, knows that he should by all rights hate Gifford, especially after he develops a crush on the star's girlfriend. But when the two finally meet, Gifford proves to be gracious and even humble, confounding Fred's expectations and transforming his contempt into infatuation.

Fred becomes an outright fan—in the original sense of fanatic—when both men wind up in New York. As Gifford scores touchdowns for the dynastic Giants, Fred loses jobs, drinks too much, and suffers rejection upon rejection as a writer. He needs football even more than booze. "The Giants were my delight, my folly, my anodyne, my intellectual stimulation," he explains. For

Fred, Gifford becomes a stand-in for his own frustrated desire for success. "He may be the only fame I'll ever have!" he confesses at one point. His investment in the halfback is so deep that Fred comes to believe himself to be, "in some magical way, an actual instrument of [Gifford's] success." On the same day that Gifford suffers a terrible concussion, Fred provokes a fight with strangers on a New York City street that leads to him being beaten down as well.

In *A Fan's Notes*, Exley brilliantly captures the status of the athlete in the fifties. White, aloof, and uncontroversial, Gifford is a tabula rasa upon which spectators can project their fantasies and aspirations. His one off-the-field appearance in the novel shows him to be wearing a "public" face even as a college student. He seems to exist only for the book's troubled narrator to use as a plat-form for his own dreams of fame. The reader is left with the feel-ing that if Frank Gifford did not exist, Frederick Exley—both the author and his protagonist—would have invented him. In some ways, this is precisely what happens.

But the author's take on the athlete is not just limited to the 1950s. He provides an indelible portrait of the desperate intensity of a fan's attachment to his hero in any era. In the focused, self-contained world of the playing field, an athlete's triumphs are amplified, and his failures can be redeemed on the very next play. It is no wonder that Fred should locate a lion's share of his own emotional life there, and not in the more complicated and frus-trating real world, with its failing marriages, lousy jobs, seedy bars, and rejection letters. Exley rightly notes that everybody who cheers an athlete's fame in some way feels that he has earned the right to take a portion of it for himself. In the narrator's case, this attachment runs so deep that Fred even "had a glimpse of [his] own mortality" when he sees Gifford lying on the playing field after being knocked unconscious. To anyone who might have told the book's feckless, drunken protagonist to get a life, he would have probably responded that he already had one—located on the gridiron where the Giants and their luminous star played.

By the time *A Fan's Notes* was published in 1968, this sort of deep identification with an impassive, iconic athlete was becoming increasingly complicated. Another revolution in the athlete's image was coming, one that would transform him into an agent of cultural as well as political and economic change. This time, the athlete would move right to the center of the West's imagination. It was an onslaught that began with the long-delayed inclusion into the professional ranks of members of an ethnic group who would provide some of the greatest athletes of all time.

CHAPTER 7

SHIRTS VS. SKINS

On the evening of July 8, 2010, LeBron James, arguably the greatest basketball talent of his generation, appeared on a live, nationally broadcast television show to announce his future plans. The hour-long program was portentously titled "The Decision." At the conclusion of what turned out to be an exceptionally awkward hour of television, James announced he would, as suspected, be leaving the Cleveland Cavaliers, where he had played for seven seasons and earned two league MVP awards but, crucially, had not won an NBA championship. His destination was the Miami Heat, where he would be joining two other top players, Chris Bosh and Dwyane Wade, to form what most observers believed would become a sporting dynasty.

The announcement provoked strong debate. To his detractors, James was the embodiment of everything that was wrong with the modern athlete. He was seen as being disloyal to his hometown and selfish in his pursuit of big bucks. He was cast as a quitter who had given up on the Cavaliers before the task of building the once-lowly team into a champion had been completed. Cleveland fans felt particularly aggrieved. They had invested emotional capital in him, and here he was, like some shady property developer, cutting and running before they could start earning dividends. More maddening still was the manner in which the decision was announced, with James grandiosely letting the world know, "I'm going to take my talents to South Beach and join the Miami Heat."

James had his defenders as well. He had, after all, spent seven seasons playing for Cleveland, a period as long as many pro careers. Loyalty, after all, was not exactly common in an era when owners moved entire franchises without consulting fans. In terms of money, James almost certainly could have received a bigger contract going to the New York Knicks, as many assumed he would. He wanted to be part of a dynasty, like Michael Jordan, Magic Johnson, and Larry Bird before him. And he had come to understand that this was not going to happen in Ohio.

At the end of the day, James was simply demonstrating how a top athlete conducts himself in the 21st century. Sports is a business. Players are free agents. They honor their contracts and then they go shopping for a better deal. A fan's reaction to James said less about his opinion of that particular player than how he viewed the changing nature of the athlete himself. The whole event should have been nothing more than grist for the mill of call-in sports chatter, in which the actions of top athletes are passionately debated for short periods before the next topic is introduced.

Then things got ugly. "The Decision" took on a whole new dimension two months later when James was asked if he thought race was a factor in the backlash against him. "I think so at times," he replied. "It's always, you know, a race factor." His answer stunned white sportswriters and fans. Many thought this was simply another example of posturing by the superstar. The controversy was about money, loyalty, and branding. But race? They simply could not see it. The situation grew more heated when the civil rights campaigner Jesse Jackson weighed in after Cavaliers owner Dan Gilbert wrote an open letter to Cleveland fans accusing James of narcissism, cowardice, and treachery. In response, Jackson said Gilbert possessed a "slave master mentality" that made him see his former star as a "runaway slave."

The rapidity with which the conversation had turned to race was remarkable. No mainstream journalist had cast the move in ethnic terms. No white teammates had been heard muttering epithets. And it was not as if there was any significant difference in the racial composition of the two teams involved. The Cleveland head coach for most of James's tenure had been African American; owners of both teams were white. And yet with one comment, attention turned to the matter of race. James's black defenders, like his business manager Maverick Carter, felt compelled to support the player's suggestion of racism; white journalists who had criticized James were forced to justify their motives.

Seen from the viewpoint of history, James's and Jackson's assertions become much more understandable. The notion of team loyalty has a complicated past when applied to the black athlete in America. The white athlete, after all, usually wears only one uniform. He is a Celtic or a Red Wing or a Colt. If he makes the Olympic team, that uniform bears the American flag and the letters "USA." The black athlete, however, has always worn two uniforms. There is the one given him by the team he plays for. And then there is a deeper, more permanent uniform—his skin. The first uniform, as James demonstrated, can be exchanged, often to the player's benefit. The second uniform is for keeps. It will not change if its owner is traded away or if he signs a long-term contract. It will remain the same if he hits the cycle in a World Series game or lets an easy grounder go through his legs. Not only can it never be altered, but it often trumps the mascot or flag on the outer uniform. Black athletes from Jesse Owens and LeBron James have always understood this, even if their white critics and fans have not.

Shirts versus skins. It is the oldest, simplest way to identify teams on a playground. One side keeps their shirts on, the other strips them off. Harmless in itself, the practice also suggests something that has been going on throughout history. In many athletic competitions, there have been the privileged participants—the shirts—and then there have been skins, the players who have the chips stacked against them. In the Colosseum, the skins were the Syrian, Saxon, Ethiopian, and Gallic prisoners who were slaughtered for the amusement of the shirts, those Romans whose togas shielded them from the blistering sun. In 19th-century America, the skins could be the Irish who used boxing as a way of escaping their ghettos. A few generations later, it was the turn of the Jews to be the skins as they too used sports as one way of fleeing their own ghettos. In the West Indies, the skins were the black cricketers who were forced for decades to play on teams that could only be captained by a shirt—a white person of British descent.

Nowhere has the shirt-versus-skin dynamic been played out more powerfully than with black athletes in the United States. Their skin has always placed expectations on them above and beyond anything demanded of white players. In the era of segregation, they were required simply to be invisible, unless, like Louis or Owens, they were drafted into national service. In the period after

Jackie Robinson broke the color barrier in professional team sports, they were expected to be stoical, to endure abuse no player of Italian or Irish ancestry would countenance. During the sixties, they were seen to be rebellious, symbols of an emerging black power that produced more than just home runs, touchdowns, or swishes. More recently, African American athletes were expected by many to bring a "gangsta" style to the game, a complicated mixture of flamboyance, aggression, and defiance personified by figures like basketball's Allen Iverson. LeBron James may indeed have simply been playing the race card when he claimed that he felt there was a racial undertone to the hostility being directed his way. But no one with any understanding of the black athlete can deny that this is a card that has been placed in the hand of every black competitor since the first plantation owner forced the first slave to ride, run, or box for his pleasure and profit.

While dark-skinned athletes have been figures of fear and fascination since antiquity, their story starts in earnest where so much of the modern athlete's history truly begins—in Victorian England. As we have seen, the British used sports as a means of spreading their Empire. The public school boys who went on to become colonial administrators were well prepared to serve as coaches for the native people they had conquered. In colonized regions of India, the Caribbean, and East Africa, British officers and diplomats organized cricket matches and soccer games with the same care they lavished on building hospitals or restructuring the local economy. True, part of this effort was motivated by a desire to turn these often-hostile environments into places that would be little pieces of England. Games could be whites only. But administrators also saw sports as an important tool in their civilizing mission. On the simplest level, they were a means of keeping energetic young men occupied in endeavors that did not involve slitting the throats of Englishmen as they slept. There was also a deeper cultural purpose. By teaching conquered populations to replace their own games with ones that resembled those of their masters, the British believed they would be able to sever indigenous people from their traditions and indoctrinate them into the values of their colonizers. Teach them the moves and rules and manners of the Western athlete, the thinking went, and their hearts and minds would follow.

The use of the athlete for colonial purposes can best be seen during the heyday of the Raj, the name given the British administration of the area that now encompasses India, Pakistan, Bangladesh, and Sri Lanka. Although cricket began to be played in this region in the early 18th century, it truly took hold among the native population in the latter part of the following century, when newly formed clubs of local players would be pitted against one another, as well as against sides composed of British cricketers. The sport became deeply popular, especially among India's upper classes. And yet there was always an ambivalent attitude toward the game among much of the indigenous population. Its efficacy in turning Indians into Englishmen was matched by its ability to create non-white players who used the game as a means of showing up their political masters. The people of the Indian subcontinent were passionate about their cricket players, never more so than when they excelled against their political masters on the pitch. As the historian Ashis Nandy noted in his *The Tao of Cricket*, "Cricket is an Indian game accidentally discovered by the English."

Perhaps the most notable product of this alchemical mix of

race, culture, and class was K. S. Ranjitsinhji, or Ranji, who in 1896 became the first player from India to be "capped," or chosen for the English national team. He was a remarkable character who balanced an identity as a national political leader, the Maharaja Jam Sahib of Nawanagar, with an international reputation as one of the greatest batsmen of all time. Born into an ancient dynasty, Ranji took up the game while a student at Trinity College, Cambridge. Soon after graduation he began playing for England, scoring a century, the gold standard of cricket batsmen, in his first-ever test. He also became a prolific player in English county cricket. While amassing scoring totals which remain among the greatest ever, he introduced a defensive, back-footed batting style that was an innovation of the game as it was played back in his native country. Perhaps it is not surprising that a member of an oppressed people should adopt a defensive stance while dealing with his masters. What was new was the fact he used that stance to beat them at their own game. It was one of the first instances of an athlete of color infusing a white-dominated sport with a new technique and energy, a process that would be repeated on baseball diamonds, soccer pitches, and basketball courts in the century to come. As Ranji sliced through the offerings of bemused bowlers from Kent and Yorkshire, British fans might have stopped to wonder just who had conquered whom.

Native athletes often came to symbolize the forces of liberation. Take the West Indian cricketer. Although formed in the 1890s, the "Windies," the team comprising players from throughout the English-speaking Caribbean, was dominated by white players until the 1950s, even though the population of the islands was overwhelmingly of African descent. While the team did have a black captain for a single test series in 1947, it was not until the 1960s, when many of the nations of the region were attaining independence, that both the team's captain and practically all of its players were allowed to be black. The Windies went on to become the most dominant team in the world in the 1970s and 1980s under the stewardship of Clive Lloyd and Viv Richards. In one famous test series in 1976, they decimated their former colonial masters on British soil after the English captain, Tony Greig, unwisely boasted, "I intend to make them grovel." His words fueled the fire of the fearsome West Indian fast bowlers as they mowed down the English batsmen.

The contest between skins and shirts was not always a struggle for liberation. Sports could also be a fast track to assimilation for immigrant groups. With one very notable exception, this was the case in the United States during the period from the end of the Civil War through Pearl Harbor. Germans dominated baseball, while the Irish found acceptance in boxing. In the case of the latter group, the struggle had a rocky start. When the Irish began to arrive in the United States in large numbers following the Potato Famine of 1845 to 1852, they were seen by many as constituting an unprecedented threat to the national character. Unable to find work, some made a living by prizefighting. When they were pitted against "native" talent in the seamy, often illegal clubs of New York and Boston, these contests could enact the era's ethnic fears. Fighters were often explicit in their allegiances, taking nicknames like "Yankee" and "Dublin Tricks." By the beginning of the century, however, nativist paranoia had found other targets, such as the Chinese, and the Irish boxer was able to become a figure of respect and even affection.

One of the most striking examples of sports as a means of ethnic assimilation can be found in the progress of Jewish boxers in New York City in the early decades of the 20th century. The reign of Daniel Mendoza as English champion from 1792 to 1795 found an echo in the United States in the period between the two world wars, with Jews predominant not only in the ring but also in positions of management and promotion. Fighters like Benny "The Great Bennah" Leonard, Leach "The Fighting Dentist" Cross and "Slapsie" Maxie Rosenbloom came to dominate the sport. So great was the Jewish presence that Max Baer fought with a Star of David on his trunks, even though he had somewhat tenuous ties to the religion. The heavyweight contender had a Jewish father but a Catholic mother, in whose religion he was raised. It says a lot about the importance of Jews in boxing that Baer proudly identified with Judaism when, in just about any other walk of American life, an ambitious man seeking assimilation would have used a mixed upbringing to move in the opposite direction.

Another sport that provided an outlet for the energy and ambition of Jewish boys was basketball. Nat Holman was undoubtedly the greatest figure of this movement. Born in the Jewish ghetto of the Lower East Side, the undersized Holman excelled at the game through sheer determination. While still involved in a successful career as a barnstorming player, he also became head basketball coach of the City College of New York in 1920, a position he would hold until 1960. During his tenure, CCNY teams, which were often composed of mostly Jewish players, were consistently among the best teams in America, winning both the NCAA and NIT championships in 1950. Holman's lasting legacy was his development of a style of play known as city ball, which abandoned individual virtuosity to emphasize passing, dribbling, setting picks, and playing zone defense, skills which allowed the often undersized CCNY players to beat much larger opponents.

It was not, of course, all about boxing titles and national championships. Jewish athletes, like all ethnic pioneers, often found themselves facing withering bigotry. Detroit Tiger first baseman Hank Greenberg, baseball's first Jewish superstar, suffered incessant taunts throughout his career, perhaps never more virulently than when he refused to play in a game that fell on Yom Kippur during the Tiger's 1934 pennant run. (Fans seem to have forgotten that, in the spirit of compromise, he *did* play on Rosh Hashanah, the Jewish New Year, the week earlier, hitting two home runs to ensure a vital 2-to-1 win for the team.) One of the more infamous moments for American Jewish athletes came two years later, during the Berlin Olympics. At the last moment, two Jewish sprinters, Marty Glickman and Sam Stoller, were dropped from the 4 x 100 relay team just hours before the race was scheduled to be held in the swastika-draped Olympic Stadium. Although US Olympic chairman Avery Brundage claimed the move was not intended to mollify the Nazis, he could produce no alternative rationale for the switch.

The ill-treatment of Jews in Berlin was a rare instance of discrimination against athletes at the Olympics. Although Baron Coubertin and his fellow founders made it clear at the outset that they saw no place for non-Caucasian athletes in their athletic spectacle, competitors have had a habit of finding a way of using the games to foil racist agendas ever since. As early as the 1904 St. Louis Olympics, South African marathoners Jan Mashiani and

Len Tau, both of them Tswana tribesmen, became the first blacks to compete in the games. Eight years later, the Native American athlete Jim Thorpe, arguably the greatest competitor ever to take part in the Olympics, buried Coubertin's dream of establishing a forum for "the strong and hopeful youth of our white race" with a series of unforgettable performances.

Although Jesse Owens provided the signature triumph of a nonwhite athlete at the Berlin Olympics, the story of the gold and bronze medalists in the marathon at the same games is every bit as compelling. The names that were entered into the record books were Kitei Son and Shoryu Nan; the flag that flew at the ceremony was the Rising Sun of imperial Japan. Anyone closely watching the ceremony would have noticed that the medalists' heads were bowed. The cause was not humility or joy, but rather shame. The winners were in fact Sohn Kee-chung and Nam Sung-yong, Koreans who were forced to compete as Japanese by their nation's viciously racist conquerors. The ruse may have fooled (or pleased) the Olympic hosts, but back in Korea photographs of the runners were printed with the Japanese flags on their uniforms obscured, an act of defiance that led to firings and arrests, but also a widespread outbreak of national pride.

It was yet another marathoner who provided perhaps the most indelible image of a Third World athlete using the Olympics as a forum to make a liberationist statement. In Rome 1960, the Ethiopian runner Abebe Bikila, an imperial guardsman in the court of Emperor Haile Selassie, stunned many observers by running barefoot to victory along the cobbled streets of Rome's Appian Way. Bikila's emergence onto the international stage was the first example of the long line of East African runners who would come to dominate the longer distances after him. More important, he came from a nation that had been brutally colonized by the host Italians just a quarter century earlier. According to legend, Bikila made the decisive break away from his competition just as he passed the huge Axum Obelisk, which Mussolini's troops had looted from Ethiopia when the marathoner was a little boy.

At the Tokyo Games four years after Bikila's barefoot victory, another long-distance runner from a beleaguered ethnic group achieved a milestone victory. Billy Mills, an Oglala Sioux from the Pine Ridge Indian Reservation in South Dakota, seemed to come from nowhere to score a stunning upset in the 10,000 meters, becoming only the second Native American to win Olympic gold. What is all the more remarkable about the achievements of Mills and Thorpe is that they emerged from an athletic legacy that was often at odds with the victory-at-all-costs ethos of the continent's white inhabitants. As detailed by the legendary ethnographer Stewart Culin in his seminal 1907 encyclopedia *Games of the North American Indians*, athletes performed a deeply ceremonial function in the tribes of the continent's first inhabitants. Their play was almost always part of magical, shamanistic rituals. Balls, bats, and sticks were often subject to elaborate purification ceremonies before contests began, either to rid them of demons or infuse them with godly powers. While there is no doubt that Indians competed hard and with great skill, the emphasis was always on teamwork. Winning or losing was far less important than playing harmoniously. Ensuring the bounty of crops and livestock, not reaching some regional finals, was the goal. Contact sports were relatively rare, while games that relied on running were strongly emphasized. One of the games most widely documented by Culin was known by French trappers and missionaries as *jeu de la crosse* because the stick used by players resembled the crozier carried by Catholic bishops. It was played primarily among tribes of the Great Lakes and the Northeast. Contemporary accounts, some as early as the 17th century, suggest that the rules of the sport were basically similar to those of modern lacrosse. Games were, however, played on a much grander scale. Fields were 400 to 600 yards long, while hundreds, sometimes even thousands, of players could participate in a game.

Another fundamental difference was the nature of the competition itself. Culin notes that one observer of the Chippewa in 1796 Wisconsin reported that the young men of the tribe "play with so much vehemence that they frequently wound each other, and sometimes a bone is broken; but notwithstanding these accidents there never appears to be any spite or wanton exertions of strength to effect them, nor do any disputes ever happen between parties." This is in keeping with the prevailing ethos of Native American sport, which could be remarkably rough without ever being truly aggressive. Although individual players might win renown through outstanding play, there was no cult of the athlete as there had been in ancient Greece or, more pointedly, would develop among white Americans. The earth and the gods were being worshipped, not the man who scored the winning goal—if there even was a winning goal.

During the course of the 20th century, as *jeu de la crosse* became lacrosse, the game was of course stripped of its shamanistic qualities. It became popular at elite Eastern prep schools and private universities like Yale, Georgetown, and Syracuse. The sport has become so deeply associated with white privilege that when a group of Duke University players were accused of sexually assaulting an African American dancer in 2006, the case immediately set off a frenzied national conversation about the atmosphere of entitlement surrounding male athletes at many universities. While the Duke players were cleared of all charges, allegations that the game of an indigenous people has been usurped by the conquerors are harder to dismiss.

No figure is more evocative of the long conflict between shirts and skins than the black athlete in the United States. Since the days of slavery, he has been a figure of potent ambiguity to his country's white shirts. The African American has often been cast as nature's own athlete, a competitor of unique prowess and skill, capable of performing at a level that whites could only occasionally attain. At various points in the nation's history, blacks have been said to have thicker skin, greater bone density, a higher pain threshold, and longer leg muscles than their white counterparts. Balanced against these athletic virtues are accusations that he lacks the motivation, discipline, and intelligence necessary to compete at the highest level; that he is too primitive to function as a team member and too lazy to see a game through to its end. People have even sworn that blacks would never be good swimmers because they do not float. Whether they saw the black athlete as a superman or an inveterate slacker, whites for a long time were in agreement about one thing: They did not want to compete against him.

His uniqueness has usually been attributed to one reason—slavery. Nearly 400 years after the first slaves were brought to North America, that peculiar institution continues to cast its shadow over the black athlete, as seen by Jesse Jackson's rhetoric during the LeBron James controversy. In 1988, the Las Vegas oddsmaker Jimmy "the Greek" Snyder effectively ended his long career as one of America's most visible television sportscasters by infamously claiming that "the black is a better athlete to begin with because he's bred to be that way—because of his high thighs and big thighs that goes up into his back, and they can jump higher and runs faster because of their bigger thighs. This goes all the way to the Civil War when during the slave trading, the owner—the slave owner would breed his big black to his big woman so that he could have a big black kid."

What is so illuminating about Snyder's remarks, besides setting a gold standard for quasi-literate obnoxiousness, is how many myths of the black athlete they incorporate. Whatever the eugenic intentions of plantation owners in the antebellum South, black athletes are now, of course, no bigger than their white counterparts. For every Kareem Abdul-Jabbar there is a Rik Smits, the 7-foot-4 blond Dutchman who played twelve solid years for the Indiana Pacers. While it is true that black runners currently dominate the sprints in track and field, it is unlikely that slave owners, who worried constantly about their chattel escaping, would have "bred" them specially to run fast and jump high.

However wrongheaded, Snyder's comments do highlight the enduring notion that there is something different about the black athlete. There is no doubt that he brings his own peculiar strengths and weaknesses to the playing field. Often the game he plays is not quite the same as his white teammate's. But this is a state of affairs that has its foundation in history, culture, and politics, not in biology. Due to social discrimination, from slavery to

Jim Crow to the early days of integration, African Americans have long been *forced* to play a different game, to become a different sort of athlete than their white counterparts, simply to survive. The results of this relegation have been tragic, unjust, electrifying, and ultimately, heroic.

Like just about every other aspect of their native culture, the games of the Africans who were transported to America in shackles were largely wiped out by masters who wanted to eke every last bit of productivity out of their human cargo. This is not to say that slaves were invariably discouraged from being athletes. Exceptions were made when profits could be had. Plantation owners would select their most athletically gifted slaves and enter them into boxing, running, rowing, and horse-racing competitions against rival plantations. These were usually the occasion of frenetic wagering. In an echo of their predecessors in the gladiatorial ring, some of these slaves competed for manumission. This was the fate of one of the few slave athletes of whom we have a record—Tom Molineaux. After boxing his way to freedom from his Virginia plantation, Molineaux became the ultimate journeyman fighter. He first tried his hand in New York, though prejudice and the constant fear of a return to bondage caused him to make his way to England, where he eventually earned a title bout in 1810 against the British champion, Tom Cribb. It turned out to be an epic contest held in cold, wet conditions. The former slave appeared to have his opponent on the ropes, only to be denied victory when the large local crowd, inspired by a mix of nationalism and racism, invaded the ring, preventing the referee from stopping the contest. Cribb was able to recover sufficiently to defeat the exhausted American challenger, a victory he repeated in a rematch the following year.

Another fighting slave we know about is Frederick Douglass, though his title bout took place in a considerably less public, and potentially far more dangerous, arena. Sent to work for Edward Covey, a poor farmer with a reputation for "breaking" independently minded slaves, the 16-year-old Douglass recounts in his autobiography that he eventually tired of the whippings and wound up fighting his master. "From whence came the spirit I don't know—I resolved to fight." A two-hour contest ensued that Douglass eventually won. For the remainder of his time with Covey, Douglass was not touched. Nor was he prosecuted, probably because the vicious overseer did not want it to get out that he had been beaten by a 16-year-old boy. It was, Douglass later wrote, "the turning point in my career as a slave. It rekindled the few expiring embers of freedom, and revived within me a sense of my own manhood." Four years later he fled, and remained free for the rest of his life. Before slavery had been abolished, this leading black figure of the 19th century had shown how a feat of physical prowess could be the central avenue of a black man's deliverance from oppression.

The most successful black athletes during the 1800s were, without doubt, jockeys. Horse racing was the most popular sport in America before the turn of the 20th century, drawing crowds approaching 100,000 for big races. And blacks, whether freemen or slaves, were more often than not the riders. For instance, they comprised 13 of the 15 riders in the first Kentucky Derby in 1875. That same year, a 14-year-old named Isaac Murphy rode in his first race. He would go on to become the most successful jockey of his era, earning upward of $20,000 a year, a fortune at that time. Murphy's downfall, however, would prove characteristic of the trajectory of the black athlete in America. As the earning potential and visibility of all jockeys increased, white riders began to look for ways to crowd out black competitors. When racetrack shenanigans such as boxing in black riders proved unsuccessful, whites formed the Jockey Club in 1894, which explicitly excluded blacks. An already discouraged Murphy died two years later, not yet 40. Within a decade, his brethren had also lost their opportunities to ride.

A similar scenario played out in boxing, with black fighters increasingly denied the chance even to enter the ring. And it was not simply a matter of an unwillingness to share winnings. Like the overseer Covey, white boxers did not want to risk the immense loss of face that would follow a defeat by a black opponent. The case of Peter Jackson illustrates the fate of black boxers during the latter part of the 19th and the early years of the 20th centuries. The grandchild of slaves, Jackson was born in the Caribbean but moved to Australia as a child. He began boxing as a way of escaping the drudgery of working on the docks. He became an Australian and British Commonwealth champion, and then defeated "Old Chocolate" Godfrey for the World Colored Heavyweight Championship in 1888. But he never got a chance to fight the noncolored world champion, John L. Sullivan, who famously stated that he would never fight a black man.

Some black fighters, however, would simply not be denied. Joe Gans, a lightweight boxer even the most prejudiced observers grudgingly admitted was the most outlandishly talented pugilist of his era, was only given a title shot after being forced to throw several high-profile fights against white fighters. The most infamous of these dives, against Terrible Terry McGovern in Chicago in 1900, was so blatant that it caused boxing to be banned in that city for the next quarter century. Gans was finally given a title shot in 1902 and did not squander it, knocking out the reigning champ in the first round. He remained on top until tuberculosis ended his career in 1908.

That same year, the heavyweight championship was won by a boxer who would go on to become the most polarizing athlete in American history. Born in Texas to former slaves, Jack Johnson worked his way up through the heavyweight ranks with a unique style that, like that of his contemporary Ranji, relied on a strong defense and strategic counterpunching. In a time when blacks were routinely associated with pure power and little else, Johnson was already toppling stereotypes. He knew that he had to win to advance in the heavyweight ranks, but he also understood that he could not win by *too much* or else whites would be unwilling to risk humiliation. In the early part of his career, he carried more white fighters than the nation's growing railroad system. He would also conduct boisterous conversations with ringside spectators during the course of a bout, making sure that everyone got their money's worth for an evening's entertainment. Even so, Johnson was almost denied his chance. Like Sullivan before him, the reigning champion Jim Jeffries refused to give a black man a shot at the title, even though he had gladly fought Peter Jackson on his own way to the top.

Johnson had to wait for a new champ, Tommy Burns, to be crowned and then chase him to Australia to get his chance. Like Gans, he did not squander it, handily defeating Burns in 1908. Writer Jack London's infamous call for a Great White Hope to win back the crown brought former champ Jeffries out of retirement. With the prestige of his race at stake (and a big payday in the offing), Jeffries was now more than willing to climb into the ring with a black man. In the lead-up to his 1910 "Fight of the Century" against Johnson in Nevada, he famously claimed: "I am going into this fight for the sole purpose of winning the title for whites." He barely laid a glove on Johnson, who stopped him in the 15th round. The result led to race riots that left twenty five dead, all but two of them black.

While Johnson was champion, his relationships with several white women would lead to his arrest and send him into exile in 1913. He eventually lost the crown to Jess Willard in Havana in 1915. True to form, Willard then refused to give Johnson—or any other black man—a crack at the title. It was a practice that would be continued by Jack Dempsey during the 1920s when he famously ducked the talented Harry Wills, widely considered the number one contender. In the meantime, Johnson eventually returned to the United States, and prison, in 1920, serving just under a year behind bars. Although he continued to box until 1938, he never again showed his old form.

Johnson's oft-told story is particularly compelling for what it says about the athlete's power over the public imagination. There is no doubt that his defiance, especially in sexual matters, cost him dearly. And yet he was able to hold out against racial retribution for much longer than any other black man would have during an era when lynchings were common. Indeed, there was no shortage of voices calling for Johnson to meet precisely that fate. The only reason he was allowed to fight on can be found in Jack London's call for a Great White Hope to take him down. People who hated Johnson wanted to see him whipped *in the ring*. Simply humiliating another black man in some grimy jail cell or remote clearing in the woods was not enough. Johnson's crime was too public for that. This athlete needed to be humbled. He had usurped one of the white world's premier sporting icons. It needed to be taken back from him on the most visible stage possible, not in some backwoods on a moonless night. This sense of theatrical vengeance was on full display during the fight against Jeffries, when the band had been instructed to play "All Coons Look Alike to Me" as Johnson entered the ring. This attempt at intimidation clearly backfired, as the black fighter easily dominated his white opponent. After the fight, everybody knew how Jack Johnson looked—and it was unlike anyone else, black or white.

Similarly, Johnson did those who loathed and feared him an unintentional favor by skipping the country in 1913 after being convicted on highly questionable charges. Had he simply gone to prison and relinquished the crown, his unvanquished image would have loomed over their imaginations forever. His loss in Cuba was a psychological victory for distressed whites. It swept the icon from their minds in a way that an arrest or lynching would never have done. White hegemony had been reestablished in the one area where it had always seemed most tenuous, at least when there were blacks around—athletics.

It would be fifty years before another black heavyweight champion emerged who would be able to challenge white authority as audaciously as Johnson. Muhammad Ali's insurrection would give him his own share of legal difficulties. In the meantime, black athletes often labored under a sporting apartheid that forced them to compete separately. The white establishment, having seen what could happen when a defiant black athlete was allowed to compete on a level playing field, would permit blacks into the main arena only under the most controlled of circumstances. Jesse Owens might have dominated track and field, but even those close to him made it clear that his status was provisional. His own white coach, for instance, put Owens's achievements down to the belief that "The Negro . . . is closer to the primitive than the white man. It was not long ago that his ability to sprint and jump was a life-and-death matter to him in the jungle." However great his speed, Owens could not carry his momentum from Berlin's Olympic stadium through to his retirement years in the United States, where he was forced to race against horses and dogs in sideshows to make ends meet. Although America's athletic apartheid was often unspoken, like the gentleman's agreement that kept Jews out of country clubs for so long, it was sometimes made explicit in rule books, such as in the charter of Professional Golfers' Association, which decreed in 1934 that members must belong to the "Caucasian Race."

Joe Louis was another black athlete who was reluctantly pressed into service as an icon for national pride in his 1938 fight with Max Schmeling, who had soundly beaten him two years earlier. Although Louis's path to the title, which he won in 1937, was littered with fewer obstacles than Johnson's, he nevertheless was burdened by prejudices no white fighter would ever have to endure, including a vicious whispering campaign that he was illiterate. And yet many white commentators seemed more than happy to nominate Louis to symbolically carry the Stars and Stripes into a fight that was seen as a warm-up for the escalating conflict against Nazi Germany. Blacks knew better. They understood that white support for Louis was not even skin deep. They could hear the white Americans who were rooting for Schmeling. And these did not always have a Southern accent. Despite the narrative that pitted Louis against Hitler, just as Jesse Owens had faced him two years earlier, blacks knew that many Americans could not stomach the prospect of a black man pummeling one of their own. Beneath the flags, the rules remained the same: shirts versus skins.

So it was understandable that blacks did not do much flag-waving during the celebrations following Louis's first-round demolition of the German challenger. In fact, the hours following the knockout became a spontaneous nationwide demonstration against the bigotry that had so long oppressed African Americans. Whites unwise enough to wander into places like Harlem after the final bell were liable to be given the same treatment as Schmeling. Mostly, however, black reaction was sheer joy. As the novelist Richard Wright memorably saw it:

> In Harlem . . . a hundred thousand black people surged out of taprooms, flats, restaurants, and filled the streets and sidewalks like the Mississippi River overflowing in flood time. With their faces to the night sky, they filled their lungs with air and let out a scream of joy that seemed would never end, and a scream that seemed to come from untold reserves of strength . . .

Like Owens, Louis would learn that the adulation of his white countrymen did not last long. After volunteering to serve in the Army during World War II, he found himself placed in a segregated unit for basic training. While giving boxing demonstrations, he suffered several humiliating episodes at the hands of white soldiers, including one in which he and Sugar Ray Robinson were ordered to relinquish their seats in a bus terminal by a spectacularly foolhardy white military policeman. In another incident, Louis had to use his powers of persuasion to keep his friend Jackie Robinson from being arrested for striking a racist officer. After retiring from boxing, Louis found work as a professional wrestler and an "official greeter" at Caesars Palace. For a man who had symbolically defeated Hitler, it was meager recompense indeed.

NOWHERE was athletic segregation more blatant than in the "Negro" baseball leagues in which black professionals were forced to play from 1920 until the 1950s. Before this period, black baseballers had followed the same desultory course as their fellow athletes. During Reconstruction, they were given relatively free access to the game, even though they were customarily subjected to racist abuse once the playing started. Moses Fleetwood Walker, for instance, played catcher for several teams in the 1880s, becoming the first black ever to play Major League Baseball when he suited up for the Toledo Blue Stockings of the American Association. Although he was generally regarded as one of the best catchers in the game, his skin color proved too much for figures like the legendary white manager Cap Anson, who twice refused to field teams against Walker. So deep was racism that one of Walker's own pitchers refused to accept signals from a black man, simply throwing whatever pitch he wanted and letting Walker figure it out as the ball streaked toward him. The writing was clearly on the center field wall. By 1890, blacks were unofficially banned from big league ball.

Their answer was to form a league of their own, one in which African Americans would not only fill the rosters, but also form the front office management. The foremost of these, the Negro National League (NNL), was run by Andrew "Rube" Foster, a former player and one of America's most dynamic, underappreciated entrepreneurs. One of Foster's main goals was to move beyond the practice of barnstorming, in which black clubs would roam the country in search of games against other teams. In addition to the exhaustion and inconvenience for players, this also left them utterly dependent on white owners, agents, and stadium managers. At the end of the day, the barnstorming team was little more than a bunch of hired hands who could be picked up for an afternoon's entertainment and then sent on their way by white promoters who felt no obligation to ensure their long-term financial welfare.

Foster's goal was not only autonomy for the black athlete but also some sort of control over the process of integration when it eventually came, as this visionary organizer knew it must. His dream was to have NNL teams eventually become part of the white league. It was not to be. The white power structure, led by a powerful baseball commissioner, the former Supreme Court justice and avowed segregationist Kenesaw Mountain Landis, made it abundantly clear they would never let this happen. Having white teams take the field against all-black squads was as unpalatable to him as stepping into the ring against black opponents had been to John L. Sullivan and Jack Dempsey. Foster eventually cracked under the strain. He died in a mental institution in 1930. The NNL dissolved in 1932.

Negro teams continued to compete in a variety of leagues that were less idealistic in their aspirations but did provide homes to some of the greatest players of all time, including Satchel Paige, James "Cool Papa" Bell, and Josh Gibson. Negro baseball was eventually done in by Branch Rickey's signing of Jackie Robinson to the Brooklyn Dodgers in 1947. Although perhaps not the greatest black player of his generation, the gifted Robinson was judged to be the one possessing the sort of strength of character that would allow him to endure the vicious racism to which he was subjected by fans and fellow players. Other stars followed, including the 42-year-old Paige, who in 1948 became one of the oldest rookies in baseball history. The rationale for black leagues had vanished, as did the chance for black control of teams. A talent-starved white establishment might have been ready for black players; accepting black owners and managers was a different matter altogether.

As other professional sports followed suit, the era of athletic apartheid finally ended. It had been fueled, of course, by the tenets of Jim Crow, the dream of a permanent black underclass. And yet, as demonstrated by the phenomenon of Jack Johnson at the beginning of the century, there was always something else at work—the fear by whites that blacks were better than them. Not just in ways that could be measured by raw results, but in the much more important matter of providing idols for a hero-hungry public. As the athlete evolved into the central paradigm of American manhood, the white establishment understood that it had to be on guard against the very real threat that the idol would be usurped by the black man. Jack Dempsey did not duck Harry Wills because he was afraid of getting beaten. Like all boxers, Dempsey faced that fear every time he stepped into the ring. He ducked Wills because he could not be allowed to lose to a *black* man. Judge Landis did not keep Babe Ruth from facing Satchel Paige at Yankee

Stadium because he was afraid of the Bambino striking out—this happened 1,330 times in his career. Landis could not afford to have Ruth whiffed by a black man. If the athlete was to serve as an avatar for white boys, as well as a romantic fixation for their white sisters, then it simply would not do in the era of segregation to have that idol be black.

Like so many racist agendas, this apartheid of the imagination backfired. White folks knew something very special was happening in the sandlots and cement courts on the other side of town. Baseball lore is full of legends of blacks and whites meeting for secret contests, the most famous having Cannonball Dick Redding striking Ruth out three times in one game. Instead of erasing the black athlete, segregation wound up making him even more compelling to the impressionable white minds it was supposed to protect. It did this primarily by forcing him to develop one of the most influential characteristics of the African American sportsman— black style. Its roots may have been in meager resources and the need not to show up The Man, but black style also grew from the unique cultural energy and traditions of the black community. From Jack Johnson's passive-aggressive ring wizardry to Allen Iverson's crossover dribble, blacks have simply learned to play the game differently. And whites have always wanted a piece of that flair.

As with most forms of style, the one belonging to the black athlete is difficult to define, though impossible to miss. And it has evolved over the years, starting out as a sort of sly exuberance, taking on aspects of black rebellion and liberation that exploded in the 1960s, and then evolving into an uneasy dalliance with "gangsta" fashion in the 1980s and 1990s. Negro League baseball, for instance, developed a style all its own, one that relied on speed and improvisation, a kind of jazz with cleats. Black players stole bases at will; they bunted with two strikes and mercilessly razzed their opponents. Fans were left in no doubt that the men on the field were *playing* in every sense of the word. There was a joy to the game that was not always evident in the demeanor of the solemn Germans and Italians who populated the major leagues. Although one of the main reasons Jackie Robinson was chosen to integrate the game was because he was seen as unthreatening, he nonetheless brought black style to the attention of the white public every time he stole home, as did the similarly mild-mannered Willie Mays when he made his basket catches. Sugar Ray Robinson displayed black style while fighting his famous series against Jake LaMotta, dancing and jabbing his way to victory against an opponent who relied on brute power.

The development of black style was not limited to the United States. In Brazil, soccer players of African ancestry brought a similar energy to the game. Introduced by English immigrants in the late 19th century, soccer quickly caught on, especially among poor blacks in the nation's turbulent *favelas*. As the Uruguayan critic Eduardo Galeano claims in his brilliant meditation on the sport, *Soccer in Sun and Shadow*, the game was "tropicalized" in cities like Rio de Janeiro and São Paulo. It was freed up and energized. It became a sort of dance, with roots in the music and rhythms of the ghettos. According to Galeano, early black stars "brought to the solemn stadium of whites the irreverence of brown boys who entertained themselves fighting over a rag ball in the slums." In doing so, they set the stage for one Edson Arantes do Nascimento, known to just about everyone on the planet as Pelé, to burst onto the scene at the age of 17 in the 1958 World Cup.

While black style remained somewhat muted among the first generation of African American athletes to integrate professional sports during the 1950s, by the following decade the restrictions were rapidly fading away. As society at large opened up, white fans who had been intrigued by the basket catch or secretly thrilled by the dunk shot began to demand more. They wanted to know what they had been missing all these years. They wanted to watch how the game might be played after Jimi Hendrix had performed "The Star-Spangled Banner." Sports was about to change radically. Young fans were no longer content with the comforting pacific havens their parents had found in sacred old ballparks or newly paneled dens. The athlete was about to become a revolutionary figure.

CHAPTER 8

WAR BY OTHER MEANS

A thletes had never performed like this before. Competing in the thin air of Mexico City in the autumn of 1968, the runners and the jumpers seemed to have stepped into another dimension. Records fell throughout the track and field portion of the Olympics as they had in no other games. In the 100-meter dash, Jim Hines became the first electronically timed runner to go under 10 seconds. Lee Evans also entered new territory in the 400-meter run, breaking 44 seconds for the first time to set a mark that would stand for twenty years. Most astonishingly, Bob Beamon shattered the long jump record with a leap of 29 feet 2½ inches, almost 2 feet longer than the previous world best. The jump so far exceeded expectations that Beamon landed beyond the range of the optical sighting system, forcing officials to measure the result by hand. When Beamon heard the distance, he collapsed in stunned disbelief. Many spectators and fellow competitors must have felt the same way.

So it came as no great surprise when the American sprinter Tommie Smith broke the 200-meter world record in that event's finals. The real shock came afterward, when Smith and fellow American John Carlos, who had captured the bronze medal, stepped onto the podium to receive their medals. Anyone familiar with Olympic ritual could see that there was something unusual about how the men were dressed. Their motley costumes made them look as if they had simply thrown on anything at hand back at the Olympic Village. In fact, the two black athletes had carefully chosen attire that was rich in symbolism. Both went shoeless to represent the poverty that continued to afflict their people a century after emancipation. Smith wore a black scarf around his neck as a token of racial pride, while Carlos wore beads to commemorate blacks who had been lynched. Both men wore black gloves, Smith on his right hand, Carlos on his left. They had intended to both wear right-handed gloves, but had remembered to bring only one pair.

Any doubt that something unusual was in the air was dispelled the moment the flags were raised and the national anthem began to play. Smith and Carlos bowed their heads and raised their gloved fists in the Black Power salute that had become familiar in the past few years. It was a remarkably potent image. Even the white Australian silver medalist Peter Norman had been moved to join the protest after hearing the plans of his fellow athletes. At the last moment, he pinned to his sweat suit a badge of the Olympic Project for Human Rights, the organization headed by the American sociologist Harry Edwards that was leading the civil rights protest Smith and Carlos had just so graphically highlighted.

The backlash against the sprinters was immediate, and it was virulent. International Olympic Committee (IOC) president Avery Brundage ordered Smith and Carlos suspended from the games and banned from the Olympic Village. A black fist raised in peaceful protest, it seemed, was a much more disruptive act to Brundage than a white hand giving the Nazi salute, a gesture the most powerful figure in the Olympic movement had readily countenanced in Berlin three decades earlier. The United States Olympic Committee initially refused to punish their athletes, though quickly gave in when Brundage threatened to have the entire American track and field team sent packing. Even Norman, a devout Christian who would use the ensuing publicity to criticize his own country's racist policies toward Aboriginal people, felt the establishment's wrath. He earned an official reprimand from the Australian sports authorities, who would later leave him off the national squad for the 1972 Munich Games.

It was Smith and Carlos, however, who really felt the heat. Both men were subjected to a barrage of criticism. Bill Toomey, the white American decathlete who had just won the gold medal, claimed that the actions of his teammates were "a shame and a disgrace." The Associated Press reporter at the scene wrote that "the stadium rocked with boos and cat-calls and some of the spectators made thumbs-down gestures as they would to a Mexican matador preparing for the kill," though the journalist's objectivity might be reasonably questioned, since elsewhere in his report he called the protest a "Nazi-like salute." Perhaps the most memorable criticism came from a young Brent Musburger, who would later become one of America's most well-known sportscasters. In solidarity with his colleague from the AP, he called the two sprinters "black-skinned storm troopers" in a newspaper column published soon after the protest.

The strength of the reaction did not stem simply from the fact that the protest involved the Black Power movement. After all, it was 1968. Protests were becoming common occurrences at just about any event where young people found a platform. Rather, establishment anger grew from the fact that Smith and Carlos had knowingly infiltrated one of the most sacred spaces in all of sports in order to generate their revolutionary tableau. Pop music idols and movie stars could protest all they wanted. It was almost expected of them. The athlete, however, was too powerful and too sacred a figure to be allowed to indulge in this sort of apostasy. Spectators had been conditioned to see the Olympic athlete as being above politics, operating in a world where competition was fair and ennobling, and all men were brothers. Now, in front of hundreds of millions of people, Smith and Carlos had desecrated the temple. And they had done it to devastating effect, creating an image that utterly subverted what Brundage and the other conservative powers running the show intended to display. Instead of taking their place in that great mural of humble, triumphant athletes adorned with precious metals and olive branch crowns, they were presenting a startling image that evoked poverty, murder, and defiance. This is why it was so important to these blazingly fast men that their protest was as silent and immobile as those great ancient Greek statues of athletes, *Discobolus* and *The Pugilist at Rest*. If they had moved, if they had shouted or chanted, they would have shattered their brilliant icon. As it was, they made it immortal.

During the period that ran roughly from the inauguration of John F. Kennedy to the fall of Saigon, the athlete became deeply embroiled in the social eruptions that reverberated across the United States and much of the Western world. The prosperity America experienced during that era meant people had more leisure time to attend games or watch them on television. Networks, hungry for advertising revenue, devoted more time to sports, confident that these programs would generate ever-higher ratings. Newspapers continued to spill buckets of ink to report on the athlete and discuss his significance, though now they were joined by monthly magazines such as *Esquire* and *The New Yorker*, who employed some of the nation's best novelists and essayists to write about figures like Bill Bradley and Muhammad Ali. Aided by this overheated media, mega-events like the World Series, the Olympics, and the Super Bowl came to dominate the public imagination for weeks at a time.

Given his greatly enhanced profile, the athlete inevitably became a pawn in the evolving contest between the establishment and the forces of change. For conservative politicians, media barons, sports franchise owners, and old-school fans, the athlete helped guard a culture they saw to be under dire threat. He was an avatar of the old-fashioned values of wholesomeness, godliness, and duty. He was clean-cut. Some voices on the left countered by launching attacks against the athlete, seeing him as a tool of the mass media and the military-industrial complex. His fans, in this view, were hypnotized dupes. In his 1967 essay "Education After Auschwitz," the German philosopher Theodor Adorno claimed that modern sports "can promote aggression, brutality, and sadism, above all in people who do not expose themselves to the exertion and discipline required by sports but instead merely watch: that is, those who regularly shout from the sidelines." Elsewhere, Adorno argued that the ultimate value of modern sports is to "train men all the more inexorably to serve the machine." It was bread and circuses all over again, only the citizens of this New Rome did not even have to leave the comfort of their wood-paneled dens for their sensibilities to be deadened by athletic spectatorship. Modern fans had become stupefied by the athlete and his spectacles, making them ripe pickings for Madison Avenue hucksters. As Jack Scott, the radical track coach who would later help the fugitive heiress Patty Hearst flee the FBI, stated his 1971 manifesto *The Athletic Revolution,* "athletic contests . . . bring some temporary excitement and meaning into the often meaningless, lonely lives of all too many middle-aged American males. A dull, insignificant job can be more easily endured if one is able to spend evenings and weekends watching exciting sports events."

This skepticism was, if anything, more intense among members of the antiwar movement, who saw the violence of modern competition as a means of preparing participants, whether players or spectators, for war. As a solution to this corruption of the athlete, some leftist educators and sociologists proposed a complete restructuring of sports, in which professional leagues would be abandoned for participation at a local level. The NFL and Major League Baseball would be phased out in favor of organizations where neighbors could play gentle games as a means of achieving physical fitness and learning how to get along. The hypnotized spectator would give way to the earnest participant. The outsize athlete created by the modern media would vanish. In his place would appear millions of citizens engaged in recreation.

Clearly, no such thing was going to happen. The colossus that was the 20th-century Western athlete was here to stay. Accepting this, some on the left began to understand that the athlete's power and popularity could be used for their own agendas. Athletes sympathetic to social change came under pressure to use their ever-expanding visibility to speak and act. In a few cases, they brought the fight for civil rights or peace in Vietnam directly onto the field of play. As seen with Smith and Carlos, these protests could come at considerable expense to their own careers.

The most galvanizing and divisive athlete of the era was undoubtedly Muhammad Ali. These days, when his iconic presence is so overwhelming as to be monolithic, it can be difficult to remember how many different Alis his contemporaries were forced to deal with during his first decade in the public eye. He was as protean a figure to his fans as he was to his opponents. His rapidly evolving persona often seemed to be following the same seismic contours as the sixties themselves. First, there was handsome, clean-cut Cassius Clay, the talented young boxer who won a gold medal for his country in the 1960 Rome Olympics, then turned professional with the backing of a syndicate of white southern businessmen. There was the brash young champion who delighted fans by spouting anthology-worthy poetry, only to terrify them by changing his name and allying himself with the Nation of Islam. It was during this period that Ali's public pronouncements became explicitly critical of whites, going so far as to advocate the separation of the races espoused by his adoptive church.

And then came the Vietnam War. Unlike black athletes who came before him, Ali had no intention of taking up arms for a nation he believed to be oppressing him. "I ain't got no quarrel with the Viet Cong," he famously remarked. "No Vietnamese ever called me nigger." Ali's refusal to be inducted into the Army brought about yet another transformation. He became the most famous draft resister in the nation. What was most galling to the war's supporters was how Ali directly subverted so many of the stereotypes they used to bludgeon the conflict's opponents. His stature as an athlete inoculated him against the usual slanders. He was not a hippie or a pampered college student; his roots were certainly among the working class. Most of all, he was not a coward. He was, in fact, demonstrably brave, having twice faced Sonny Liston, one of the hardest punchers in the sport's history. When he refused to step forward in that Texas induction center in 1967, Ali laid down a new standard for what was politically viable for the athlete.

Besides energizing the antiwar movement, Ali's protest also completed a process he had started the first time he did the "Ali shuffle" or talked trash about an opponent. It moved black style into the dead center of the athletic mainstream, albeit in a more challenging manner for many white spectators. Brash, flash, lucid, playful, defiant, capable of encapsulating epic rage and then defusing it with a single facial flex, Ali was everything his impassive forebearers like Joe Louis and Jackie Robinson were not. In fact, he made clear his lack of regard for some of the black athletic legends who had preceded him. When Louis criticized his refusal to go to war, Ali called the ex-champion an Uncle Tom, the most harmful insult one black man could sling at another during these tumultuous times. Ali resembled no boxer more than Jack Johnson. This time, however, a significant and powerful section of the white public was ready to support him. After being sentenced to prison (his conviction was later overturned) and stripped of his title, Ali became iconic, an apotheosis made explicit with *Esquire* magazine's epochal 1968 cover "The Passion of Muhammad Ali," which posed the boxer as Saint Sebastian, the Christian martyr and patron saint of athletes. Showing his body riddled with arrows, his head thrown back as if he had just been caught with an uppercut, the photo cemented Ali's status at the forefront of a counterculture that was rapidly gaining equal footing with the mainstream. Black style was no longer primarily a means of entertainment whose protest was deeply coded. It could also be a means of explicit rebellion against the status quo.

Other athletes followed suit. Although most of them lacked Ali's political convictions and his sheer bravery, they rivaled his sense of style and his outlaw energy. The change could be seen at the most obvious levels. Hair grew longer, lapels widened, street shoes started coming with elevated heels. Statements to the press were no longer delivered in guarded monotones, but were peppered with slang. In basketball, Walt "Clyde" Frazier of the New York Knicks played with a fluidity that seemed to come from the same city streets as his colorful clothes. Lingering beneath the bold fashion and new attitudes was a sense that these men were no longer necessarily playing the game solely on the white man's terms. In baseball, the 1967 St. Louis Cardinals became the first World Series champions to be dominated by the black style that had been born in the Negro Leagues and given a radical jolt by the insurrection happening in America's ghettos. Led by a trio that included the fiercely defiant pitcher Bob Gibson, the base-stealing wizard Lou Brock, and the smoothly versatile center fielder Curt Flood, the Cardinals seemed a far cry from the platoons of lantern-jawed, crew-cut white men who had dominated play just a few years earlier. In football, Jim Brown ran like no one before him, breaking NFL records with a style that combined explosive power with smooth locomotion. Like other black athletes, Brown pursued a movie career after his 1965 retirement, but instead of the stiff patriotic fare of Joe Louis or the inspirational biopic created for Jackie Robinson, Brown starred in crowd-pleasing hits like *The Dirty Dozen*, as well sexy, edgy movies such as *100 Rifles*, which cast him in one of Hollywood's first interracial sex scenes with Raquel Welch.

It was not just black athletes who seemed to take inspiration from Ali's countercultural stance. Joe Namath, the quarterback for the New York Jets, became the most visible white icon of athletic nonconformity. After a college career at the University of Alabama under the tight supervision of the archconservative head coach Bear Bryant, the preposterously gifted Namath was set loose on New York City in 1965, complete with the largest salary in pro football history. He went on to break several passing records but also shattered conventions by growing long sideburns, wearing white shoes on the field and fur coats off it, and engaging in the type of braggadocio characteristic of Ali when he publicly guaranteed a victory over Baltimore in the 1969 Super Bowl. "Broadway Joe" made good on his promise with a famous win, only to clash with authorities over his freewheeling personal life, most notably after NFL commissioner Pete Rozelle ordered him to divest his interest in a Manhattan nightclub named Bachelors III. Namath abruptly quit the game, leading to a compromise with the NFL that allowed him to retain some contact with the nightlife he loved. He went on to shave off his trademark Fu Manchu moustache and famously don pantyhose in television commercials. Like Brown, his film debut also had a countercultural edge to it, with Broadway Joe appearing as a member of a motorcycle gang called "The Heads" in the 1970 bomb *C.C. and Company*.

It could be argued that Namath's status as a countercultural athlete went no deeper than his clothes and facial hair (or his acting ability). After all, clashing with the authorities over the right to run a meeting spot for swinging singles is not on the same level as risking five years in a federal penitentiary for refusing to take part in a war in which thousands of your countrymen are dying. Namath's post-retirement career as a broadcaster and guest star suggests that a deeply conventional heart may have been beating beneath that fur coat. The immensely popular middle-distance runner Steve Prefontaine, who set numerous American records during the early 1970s, was an athlete whose long hair, drooping moustache, and hard-charging style made him look as if he might have stepped straight from the front lines of a campus antiwar protest. In fact, "Pre" was a single-minded competitor whose only notable political act was to protest the ban on athletes being paid for competing in big, money-making track meets.

In the United Kingdom, the Northern Irish soccer player George Best of Manchester United, the European Footballer of the Year in 1968, looked very much like a long-haired rebel out to shake up a hidebound old game, though in the end his countercultural significance amounted to little more than a few new nightclubs, a string of broken hearts, and some epic bar tabs. Bill Walton became well known for his flowing red hair, vegetarianism, antiwar rhetoric, and enthusiasm for the Grateful Dead while an All-American basketball player at UCLA in the early 1970s, but it was chronic foot injuries rather than any political stance that limited his long career in the NBA. He would go on to become an unadventurous mainstream sportscaster who would speak out against basketball's next generations of rebels, such as the 1991–1992 "Fab Five" of the University of Michigan, who so emphatically brought the black style to college basketball.

The era's most lasting athletic liberation movement was led

by two black men. Their names were not Smith and Carlos, however, but Haywood and Flood. Their struggles were not about protesting nuclear weapons, segregation, world hunger, or the conflict in Indochina. They were, however, fighting for a certain kind of freedom—the freedom of the athlete to exercise control over a career that had long been the property of the team for which he toiled. In an era of tumultuous social, sexual, and political change, it was a showdown over contracts that would prove to be the athlete's most enduring revolution.

Through the 1960s, Curt Flood had established himself as one of the best center fielders in the game of baseball. He could do it all—run, hit, catch, and throw. He had considerable flair and yet was also a famously steadfast leader. As captain of the St. Louis Cardinals, one of the most storied franchises in baseball, he had led the team to three National League pennants and a World Series victory in 1967. Fans in St. Louis, where he played for twelve years, loved him. And he loved them right back. The city was his home. In fact, some commentators credited Flood and the other black stars on the Cardinals with helping keep the city calm during the explosive summer of 1967, when so many other American cities went up in flames.

So it came as a considerable shock to Flood when, in 1969, he was abruptly traded to the Philadelphia Phillies. He had no say in the matter. A player almost never did. Baseball's reserve clause effectively tied him to the team that had originally signed him for as long as its owners wanted him, while also giving the owners the right to trade him whenever they felt like it. Developed in the 19th century and endorsed by the Supreme Court in 1922 in one of its most bizarre decisions, the clause meant that a player had only two choices once he had signed with a team. He could do as told. Or he could sit it out until released from his contract, cutting off his paychecks and threatening his career with oblivion. Flood, who had no affection for either the Philadelphia team or its notoriously truculent fans, decided to sit it out. In a letter to baseball commissioner Bowie Kuhn, he stated that he would not be treated as "a piece of property to be bought and sold irrespective of my wishes." Elsewhere, he suggested a plantation mentality was at work in baseball and professional sports as a whole, in which players, black and white, were seen as little more than slaves. When his complaint was ignored, he abruptly retired from the game and brought a lawsuit that wound up going all the way to the Supreme Court. Flood was clearly right. Baseball's labor practices did indeed violate antitrust laws. But the court narrowly voted against him. In his majority opinion, which was laden with references to the game's storied traditions and pastoral splendor, Justice Harry Blackmun upheld baseball's antitrust practices as "an established aberration." Flood was effectively finished in the game. He moved to Europe so he could pursue a career as a painter.

But the floodgates had been opened. The injustice of the reserve clause had been laid bare. Within a few years, after being challenged by different, whiter players, it collapsed. A new incarnation of the athlete was born: the free agent. Players would no longer necessarily be associated with a single team. Joe DiMaggio would not have to be a Yankee; Frank Gifford could be something other than a Giant; George Best's nationality might force him to play for Northern Ireland in the World Cup tournament, but he did not have to do the same for Manchester United. While Flood saw his struggle as being part of the era's civil rights movement, the primary result of his crusade was to free up a very small number of talented men to become extremely rich.

At the same time Flood was trading his center fielder's glove for brushes and an easel, a similar struggle was taking place that would have an equally profound effect on college sports. In 1967, Spencer Haywood was widely seen as the top high school basketball prospect in the nation. At 6 foot 8, he moved with a power and grace that would serve as a model for subsequent nimble big men like Magic Johnson and LeBron James. He decided to play college ball at the University of Tennessee, though the deal fell apart at the last minute when the University of Kentucky's powerful coach Adolph Rupp intervened in retaliation for Haywood's decision not to play for his Wildcats. After spending a year at a junior college in Colorado, Haywood enrolled at the University of Detroit, where he became an All-American after one season.

And then he decided he was ready to turn pro. Two more years in college would bring nothing but the chance of a career-ending injury. The NBA, however, possessed a rule saying that a player could not enter the league until he had been out of high school for four years. So Haywood joined the American Basketball Association. Eager to make inroads against the NBA, the newly formed league had no problem signing young players. After a year in the ABA, Haywood felt as if he had paid his dues. In 1970 he signed with the NBA's struggling Seattle SuperSonics, who were more than happy to have such a gifted player on their roster. The league fought back, threatening to void Haywood's contract. He sued, and the same Supreme Court that had decided against Flood found in favor of Haywood. (Evidently the city playgrounds where basketball was often played did not evoke the same sense of pastoral splendor in

Blackmun and his fellow justices as those rural baseball diamonds.) Teenagers could enter the pro draft straight out of high school, which is exactly what top players like LeBron James, Kobe Bryant, and Kevin Garnett would eventually do.

Although recent rule changes have reestablished a one-year buffer between high school graduation and joining the professional game, the effect of *Haywood v. National Basketball Association* was to further free the athlete, at least in his incarnation as a basketball player, from another institution that held power over him. By the mid-1970s, the athlete could be his own man. Increasingly, she could be her own woman as well. This free agency was not just legal. It was also metaphorical. As the icon was dislocated from institutions that had once provided him with cover, his veneer began to crack. Athletes were no longer protected by long associations with a particular team. Fans were eager to see the dirt beneath the crumbling plaster. In a series of tell-all books that proliferated during this time, athletes were painted as selfish, avaricious, lecherous, and dipsomaniacal. And this was just their own teammates doing the writing. Flood's 1971 autobiography, *The Way It Is*, painted a picture of doped-up players indulging in one-night stands with groupies while on the road. Former Yankee pitcher Jim Bouton's brilliant *Ball Four* (1970) was so offensive to the powers-that-be that baseball commissioner Bowie Kuhn singled it out for condemnation. In it, Bouton frankly spoke of drug use among players, as well as the practice of "beaver shooting," or ogling women fans, from the dugout. Most controversially, he outed Yankee great Mickey Mantle as a full-blown alcoholic who would sometimes play while nursing head-splitting hangovers. The book contributed to the end of Bouton's baseball career, though it also helped him find steady work as an actor. The most famous of athlete tell-alls of this era was Lance Rentzel's autobiographical *When All the Laughter Died in Sorrow* (1972), which tried, with mixed results, to explain his career-ending arrest on a charge of indecently exposing himself to a 10-year-old girl while he was a star wide receiver for the Dallas Cowboys.

This is not to say that sporting conservatives were in retreat during this era. In fact, they labored mightily to patch any fissures in the icon. With the economy booming and television revenue mushrooming, the powerful interests who stood to profit financially and philosophically from sports needed to maintain the athlete's position as an embodiment of the ideal. They understood the value of the athletic icon, and they were not about to let it be captured by hirsute countercultural barbarians without a fight. The sentences handed down to Smith and Carlos were warning shots fired over the heads of all such protesters. After all, the two men had not taken performance-enhancing drugs or committed any crime; they had not cheated or gambled; they were not accused of taking money under the table from promoters or advertisers. They had simply raised their fists for a short period to draw attention to the indisputable fact that black people suffered terrible discrimination. And yet for this they were banned forever from the very thing at which they had already proven themselves to be among the world's best.

In this charged atmosphere, authority figures like Green Bay Packer head coach Vince Lombardi and Bear Bryant came to be seen as more than just brilliant field tacticians. They were generals in an informal national guard, guardians against the corruption of sport and society by the slackers, the quitters, and the weaklings.

In an age of personal liberation, they stressed the value of collaboration and the need for the individual to subsume himself in the greater good. (When Lombardi died, President Richard Nixon eulogized him as "an apostle of teamwork.") At times, it was as if these men saw the athlete as being more directly in competition with the hippie smoking pot behind the field house than with the team facing him. Coaches at all levels could be heard wistfully hoping for the day when they could get these longhairs on the practice field for an afternoon's workout so they could subject them to some good old-fashioned discipline.

The most visible champion of the athlete as an embodiment of conservative values was Nixon himself. For him, the athlete was a crucial member of the "silent majority" of citizens who were appalled at the decline of American culture. An earnest if not particularly gifted football player at Whittier College in the 1930s, Nixon would roll out the rhetoric of sports at any available opportunity during his presidency. He understood that anything he could do to make voters think of him as an athlete, or at least an ardent fan, would help win him votes. For instance, as part of his strategy of wooing Southern Democrats who were disillusioned with their party's stance on civil rights, Nixon took an active role in promoting Arkansas or Texas for the 1969 national college football championship, much to the dismay of Joe Paterno, coach of an undefeated Penn State team. Nixon also let it be known that he spent the afternoon watching college football as up to 500,000 protesters gathered in Washington for the Moratorium to End the War in Vietnam. He would famously give advice to coaches before big football games, most notably George Allen of the hometown Washington Redskins. The commander-in-chief's meddling eventually earned him a public rebuke from veteran Redskin quarterback Billy Kilmer. Nixon's most notorious appropriation of the athlete's identity for political purposes came in his use of sports jargon to name controversial military actions such as Operation Linebacker, the intensive 1972 bombing campaign against North Vietnam.

Nixon and his fellow conservatives saw the athlete as more than just an ally in their fight against antiwar protesters, countercultural rebels, and East Coast intellectuals. They also saw him as a soldier in the Cold War. The athlete was not just a symbol of enemies within; he could also be pressed into service against foreign foes. Because vast arsenals of nuclear weapons made direct conflict impossible, the United States and the Soviet Union were constantly looking for proxy conflicts to play out their mutual aggression. Events as unalike as the Fischer-Spassky world chess championship in 1972 and the Arab-Israeli War of 1973 were seen through the lens of the struggle between East and West. Given this tense atmosphere, it is inevitable that the athlete became caught up in the war. Boxing rings, running ovals, hockey rinks, and basketball courts became surrogate battlefields.

The Soviets were slow to deploy their athletes to the front lines in order to prove the superiority of their system over the West. In the years between the Russian Revolution and the end of World War II, the athlete was seen by communist ideologues to be a decadent figure, self-aggrandizing and reeking of bourgeois frivolity. Far better, they decreed, to put one's physical energy into becoming a Stakhanovite laborer, an iconic figure based upon the exploits of a miner named Alexei Stakhanov, who in 1935 broke the Soviet record by extracting over 100 tons of coal from the earth during a single shift. This use of individual strength for the common good became the ideal. If a good Russian had energy to burn, he or she should use it to build a better communist state, not to win medals or gain individual glory in some insignificant sporting event.

Things changed after World War II. As the Cold War heated up, Stalin came to understood the value of the athlete in his struggle against the West. If the sportsman could be conscripted into the cause and made to compete for the greater good, then he would no longer be a decadent figure. And it was obvious to Stalin that the battle must be played out at the Olympic Games. This provided the Russians with a level playing field, by ensuring that his American foes would not be able to draw from their valuable pool of professional sportsmen. The race to build the perfect Soviet athlete was on.

Despite the staggering losses of the Great Patriotic War, precious resources were poured into the mission. The Ministry of Sport, which by no accident was part of the regime's propaganda apparatus, took a scientific approach to the task. Sports were encouraged in the nation's schools, with any child who demonstrated exceptional ability being sent to special athletic academies, where they underwent an intense program of physical and psychological training. If this experiment in human engineering meant separation from families and native cultures, then so be it. There was a war on.

The results were astonishing. In the Helsinki Olympics of 1952, the first in which Soviet athletes participated, they won 71 medals, 22 of them gold, a tally that was second only to the mighty Americans. Four years later, they were the top medal-winning nation in the world. In the Winter Olympics, their performances were equally impressive. The Russians also began to dominate individual sports such as men's ice hockey, where the Soviet team demolished Canada 7 to 2 to win the 1954 world championship, starting a four-decade run in which they would be nearly invincible.

Much of this success came in sports that had a long tradition in the nations of the Soviet Union. Great strides were also made in those in which there was little American competition, like weight lifting and gymnastics. But occasionally Soviet athletes were able to break through in events that were seen as the domain of their US rivals. The great Ukrainian long jumper Igor Ter-Ovanesyan was a prime example. Although he was consistently bested by the American Ralph Boston in the early part of a career that spanned five Olympics, Ter-Ovanesyan and his coaches focused relentlessly on his technique, allowing the jumper to eventually beat Boston and twice break the world record. A similar program was put in place for another Ukrainian, the sprinter Valeri Borzov. His coaches at the Kiev Institute of Physical Culture studied films of great sprinters of the past, then came up with a training program in which Borzov would painstakingly reproduce the motions of those sprinters from the starting gun to the tape. The result was a gold medal in the 100 meters in the 1972 Munich Olympics, though admittedly Borzov was also helped by a bit of luck when the two leading American runners missed their quarterfinal heats due to a scheduling error. Space was not the only place where the Russians saw themselves as in a great race with the Americans.

During this era, the Cold War athlete could be found in other countries as well. Castro's Cuba, another nation with a highly centralized training system, produced a string of superb athletes, most notably the fearsome heavyweight Teófilo Stevenson, who many believed was every bit the equal of contemporaries like Ali, George Foreman, and Joe Frazier. No one will ever know for sure, however, since Stevenson steadfastly refused to have anything to do with the decadent American fight game.

No nation was more dedicated to the task of engineering the socialist athlete than East Germany. With a population only a fraction of the size of the United States or the Soviet Union, the DDR was able to create waves of super-athletes through a system that would start training children as young as 5 in specialized schools, where they attended classes ten hours a day, six days a week, right up until graduation from Hochschule für Körperkultur, or sporting universities. Eventually, this system would come to depend upon illegal doping of epic proportions, but in its early "clean" years, when the reliance was on rigorous coaching and unswerving discipline, the results were a testament to the sort of athletes who can be produced by a concerted national program.

Socialist programming was not without its victims. Some athletes can be engineered; others require the freedom to improvise. While we know the names of great athletes who thrived under the Soviet-led system, it is impossible to know how many potential world beaters were crushed by it. One name we do know is Czechoslovakia's Emil Zátopek, perhaps the greatest long-distance runner of all time. His feat of winning the 5000 meters, the 10,000 meters, and the marathon at the 1952 Olympics remains one of the greatest athletic achievements. Unlike most other Eastern Bloc athletes, Zátopek did not benefit from a vast state support system. It is unlikely he would have even been chosen for an academy at an early age. Born in 1922, Zátopek did not show athletic promise until he was 19, when he ran in a meet at the shoe factory where he worked. He was recruited to work with leading coaches, but soon set off on his own course, devising a training regimen of such rigor that it leaves even the most hard-bitten coaches scratching their heads to this day. On the track, he would run 30 or 40 long sprints at top speed, with minimal rest. For distance workouts, he would don army boots and run mile after mile through the deep snow. If the weather was too harsh, he would simply run in place in his kitchen for hours at a time. In terms of technique, he was the anti-Borzov. The only laboratory his hunched running style could have been developed in was Victor Frankenstein's. Most notable was the look of sheer agony on his face even as he pulled away from his competitors, an expression that caused one veteran sportswriter to quip that he "ran like a man with a noose around his neck."

Although a member of the Czech communist party, Zátopek was never at ease with his government. In fact, he almost missed the 1952 Helsinki Games when a fellow runner was banned by the party for political reasons. Zátopek staged a one-man boycott, forcing the authorities to back down. The indomitable spirit that he had showed on the track continued to shine through even during the darkest days of state repression. In 1966, the Australian runner Ron Clarke, who held several world records during his remarkable career but had never won Olympic gold, decided to pay a visit to the great man in Prague. At the end of his stay, Clarke was given a carefully wrapped package by Zátopek, who told the Australian he must not open it until he was safely out the country. He also cryptically told Clarke "you deserve this." Thinking it might contain some secret message for people on the other side of the Iron Curtain, Clarke did as told. It was only after his plane had left Czechoslovakia that he discovered the package contained Zátopek's gold medal for the 10,000 meters. The great runner's unruly spirit finally caught up with him in 1968, when he voiced support for the Prague Spring uprising against the Soviets. Perhaps because he was retired and no longer capable of proving the supremacy of the communist system, Zátopek was stripped of his party membership and sent to work in a uranium mine.

The most memorable events of the era of the Cold War athlete were those contests in which the great geopolitical rivalries were played out in head-to-head competition, like modern-day hastiludes. The first of these did not involve the United States, but rather pitted the Hungarian water polo team against the Soviet Union at the 1956 Melbourne Olympics. Dubbed the "Blood in the Water" match, it came just one month after Russian tanks crushed the Hungarian uprising against the Soviet-backed regime. Taunts, kicks, and punches were freely dispensed in a game that had to be abandoned with a minute remaining after a near riot by the pro-Hungary crowd when one of that team's players was bloodied by a Russian punch. Hungary was ahead 4 to 0 at the time; they were declared the winners, and would go on to secure the gold medal. They would also remain under Soviet control for another three decades.

Similar retribution was enacted in 1969, when the Czechoslovakian team twice beat the Soviets in the World Ice Hockey Championships in Stockholm. The victories came just a year after the crushing of the Prague Spring and were met back home by massive demonstrations that saw sporadic attacks against Soviet forces and institutions. Once again, any sense of deliverance was short-lived. The Czech players may have beaten the Russians on the ice, but soldiers of the Red Army continued to occupy their native land.

The signature game of the Cold War came in the 1972 Munich Olympics, when the United States played the USSR for the gold medal in basketball. Even though no NBA players had ever been allowed to compete for the United States, the team had gone undefeated in Olympic play for the last thirty six years. The squad of college players kept that streak alive at Munich until the championship game against the Soviets, and looked to have scored another gold medal when they took the lead with seconds remaining. As every basketball fan over 50 knows, the Soviets were given three chances to inbound the ball by confused officials; they scored on their final attempt. The outraged Americans refused to accept their silver medals. Revenge of sorts came eight years later, when another team of American college boys were able to beat their supposedly invincible Soviet foes in the semifinals of the ice hockey competition at the Lake Placid Winter Olympics. On the podium during the gold medal ceremony, the young US players draped themselves with American flags and raised their index fingers high above their heads to indicate the supremacy of their nation. No one thought to suspend them for bringing politics into the games.

The use of Olympic athletes as proxies in an ongoing war took a much deadlier turn in Munich, when members of the Palestinian Black September terrorist organization stormed the Israeli compound, killing an athlete and a referee, then taking nine other Israelis hostage. The ensuing standoff with German authorities was played out live on television, with veteran ABC network broadcasters Jim McKay and Howard Cosell switching seamlessly from sports to news commentary. The crisis ended with the deaths of eleven Israelis, five terrorists, and a West German policeman. It also established just how potent a political symbol the athlete had become. The Palestinians understood that capturing Israeli competitors, some of whom were weight lifters and wrestlers, would constitute a major symbolic blow against the power of the Jewish state. After the massacre, the Israelis knew that they had to respond with some force, instituting a campaign of retribution that led to the assassination of many of those involved in the Black September attack. The athlete's value as a political pawn had been given a bloody, heartbreaking demonstration. Olympic Games, and indeed most other major sports competitions, could no longer be open festivals but would rather come to be ringed with the same security seen at embassies and parliaments.

For the most part, however, competition during these proxy battles remained a peaceful example of William James's moral equivalent of war. What is remarkable is how inconclusive it all proved to be. The West may have won the Cold War, but when it comes to the athlete, the victory is by no means clear-cut. These days, tennis prodigies begin training in "academies" like Nick Bollettieri's in Florida at the same age their Soviet counterparts did fifty years ago. Top sprinters are subjected to training techniques that have more to do with those lavished on Valeri Borzov than Jesse Owens. And the majority of scholarship basketball or football players at a Division I school get an education that probably more closely resembles the one received by an East German athlete in the 1960s than what Bill Bradley experienced at Princeton during the same period. Westerners who shake their heads as they look back at the engineered athletes of the Soviet empire might benefit from taking a closer look at how much of that technology goes into the formation of the hometown athletes they cheer today.

CHAPTER 9

YOU'VE COME
A LONG WAY, BABY

On July 10, 1999, before a crowd of 90,000 wildly cheering fans in Pasadena's Rose Bowl stadium, a young woman created one of the era's most iconic athletic images simply by taking off her shirt. Moments earlier, Brandi Chastain had scored the goal that allowed the US women's soccer team to defeat China in the World Cup finals. There was nothing calculated about Chastain's reaction. She was not trying to shock the old guard or make a political gesture. Her celebration sprang from the same primal impulse that has caused male soccer players to do the same sort of thing in their own moments of athletic ecstasy. As much as any other single event, Chastain's spontaneous exposure of her sports bra suggested that, after centuries in which women had been viewed as prizes or oddities in the world of sports, they were finally being accepted as simply athletes.

It had been a long struggle. In fact, the notion of a woman being an athlete was so foreign in the pre-Christian world that almost all examples of female competitors were consigned to myth. Artemis, the virgin goddess of the hunt, was an expert archer who was rarely depicted without her bow and arrows. It is highly unlikely, however, that any of the women who worshipped her would be allowed to participate in a hunt, much less an athletic contest. Pallas Athena, the goddess of wisdom, might not have possessed the physical skills of Artemis, but she was an avid supporter of mortals, particularly Ulysses, in their own games. The mythical Amazons were a race of warriors who were supposedly so passionate about their use of the javelin and bow that some were believed to have cut off their right breasts to facilitate their throwing motion. (The term *Amazon* comes from the Greek phrase *a-mazos*, or "without a breast.") And yet their prowess was seen to have nothing to do with their feminine nature. Homer referred to them as *antianeirai*, or "those who fight like men."

Foremost among these mythical female athletes was the princess Atalanta. Legend has it she was raised by bears after being left in the wilderness as a baby by her father, a powerful king who was disappointed he had not been given a son. She became a skillful hunter and a sworn virgin who would kill any man who tried to force himself upon her. After being reunited with her father, he decreed she must marry. She had no choice but to agree, though she added that a successful suitor must be able to defeat her in a footrace. As a further condition, any man who lost would be killed. Many suitors suffered that very fate until the sly Hippomenes enlisted the help of the goddess Aphrodite, who, displaying a marked lack of sisterhood, tossed golden apples at Atalanta during the race. Distracted, the princess lost both the race and her virginity.

When it came to flesh-and-blood women, Greek men were much more reluctant to accept the idea that they could join the game. No women were allowed to compete at the Olympics or any

other major athletic contest, though there is evidence that a select
few owned racehorses and chariots. In fact, most women were not
allowed even to watch the contests. Those running, grappling nude
bodies were for male eyes only. The only female known for certain
to attend each Olympic games was a priestess of Demeter, the goddess of the harvest. There is limited evidence that women did have
a competition of their own, a very modest festival that occurred
every four years. Known as the Heraia in honor of the goddess of
women, it consisted solely of footraces. There is also evidence that
the Spartans allowed women to take part in martial games alongside men. If either of these traditions did in fact occur, participants would have been among the first in a long line of faceless
female athletes, since there are no existing records of any of them.

Roman women fared little better than their Greek counterparts. True, they were allowed into the stands at the Colosseum
and other arenas, though they were forced to sit with the very
poorest men in the upper tiers. The only evidence we have of
women taking part in any sort of competition were stories of gladiatrix, or female gladiators, who would occasionally appear in
munera. It seems that their presence was intended primarily for tit-
illation or comic effect. Mevia, a gladiatrix from Ethiopia, was said
by Juvenal to have hunted boar with her breasts exposed. And then
there was the emperor Domitian and his habit of pitting women
against dwarves to spice up an afternoon's entertainment.

Perhaps the most representative story involving women and
sports in Rome is that of the empress Poppaea Sabina. She
became one of the first known victims of sports-induced spousal
abuse when her husband, the emperor Nero, kicked her to death
after she complained about his spending too much time at the

chariot races. Nero's outburst is one of the few traditions from antiquity that continues to inform women and sports. As the *New York Times* reported in 1993, and countless counselors and women's shelter employees can attest, there is a spike in instances of wife battering after big games like the Super Bowl or England's FA Cup finals.

In the Middle Ages, women were athletic prizes, not competitors. Their participation in the hastiludes was limited to having them sponsor tourneying knights. Among the common folk outside the jousting stadiums, women also used sports to catch a man, albeit more proactively than their highborn sisters. Smock races began to take place in Britain and on the European continent during this time, and would grow in popularity until their heyday in the 18th century. On the face of it, a smock race was a simple sprint involving a number of unmarried young women, with the official prize being a blouse of fine linen. Contemporary accounts and a famous painting by Thomas Rowlandson suggest that competition could be fierce. Anything seemed to go, including tripping, slinging elbows, and grabbing a competitor by the hair as she passed. Perhaps one reason for the intensity of the race was that competitors were vying for more than just a shirt. Even more than their counterparts in the hastiludes, they were taking advantage a rare opportunity to put their bodies on display for potential spouses.

The other main European folk competition involving women also appears to have been designed more for the enjoyment of beer-sodden men than as a test of actual athletic skill. We know that women's bare-knuckle boxing was very popular at pubs and beer gardens in the early 18th century, though there is evidence that it had also been happening during the Middle Ages. Most of the action took place in London. Elizabeth Wilkinson, the "Cockney Championess," was perhaps the most proficient female fighter of this era. Married to a boxer, she would occasionally join him for mixed doubles contests and was said even to have fought men. Although accounts by contemporary diarists suggest that women's boxing matches were well attended, there is little documentation of actual fights and fighters. It simply was not worth the ink. The one detail that many of these accounts do mention, however, was that women were liable to have their breasts exposed in the heat of battle.

Up until the latter decades of the 19th century, the female athlete remained a problematical figure, who was usually greeted with bemusement, condescension, or downright hostility. Among the working classes, female athletes were seen to operate in the same demimonde as prostitutes and actresses. If a respectable woman wanted to compete, she was forced to participate in "safe" recreational sports such as archery and croquet. Any time women appeared ready to break through, male authority figures were quick to put them in their places. For instance, during the latter part of the 18th century, women were initially active in the pedestrianism craze sweeping Great Britain. They were eventually discouraged, however, when doctors and clergymen expressed alarm at the effects these prolonged treks would have on the female body, despite the fact that women had already put in some impressive performances without ill effects. One competitor, unnamed of course, was reported in 1765 to have walked over 70 miles from Scotland to northern England in the course of a single day. Women, who could of course undergo the epic exertions of childbirth, were seen as too delicate to compete in a straightforward road race. It was a prejudice that proved hard to dispel: Women were not allowed to compete in the marathon at the Olympic Games until 1984.

Even recreational activities that seem like mild diversions to modern eyes could draw alarmed condemnation from the male establishment. During the bicycling craze of the 1890s, there were no end of jeremiads about the harmful effect that pedaling would have upon a woman's reproductive organs. Less comment was made about the deleterious effects of bike riding on testicles, even though these rested much closer to the rock-hard seats of those early contraptions than ovaries did. Even acceptable sports such as lawn tennis were seen primarily as opportunities for nubile young women to be in wholesome proximity to young men. Any female player who deliberately hit a shot past a man in a Victorian mixed doubles match might have won the point, though she would also have risked social defeat.

A few dedicated competitors were not so easily domesticated. In England, a "Ladies' Singles" category was added to the Wimbledon championships in 1884. Lottie Dod, the daughter of a rich Cheshire cotton trader, would win the title five times between 1887 and 1893. Dod was arguably the first true all-round woman athlete and remains one the greatest competitors, male or female, of her era. Only 15 years old when she won her first Wimbledon, she was also a championship golfer, an Olympic archer, and a founding member of England's national field hockey team. All of this accomplished while being forced to perform in heavy, layered clothing that would have made the act of rushing the net a task of Houdini-like proportions. Despite these restrictions, women athletes continued to edge toward the mainstream. Following England's lead, France and the United States began allowing them to compete in their respective national tennis championships by the end of the century. Play was limited, however, by rules that stipulated women must serve underhand, as the motion of an overhand serve led a woman to all manner of indecent posturing.

Women were also starting to find their way onto America's baseball diamonds. In 1875, a tournament between the Blondes and the Brunettes was held in Springfield, Illinois. (In the opening game, the Blondes eked out a 42-to-38 win in the six-inning contest.) Beginning in the 1890s, barnstorming teams known as Bloomer Girls began to tour the nation, looking for games against men's teams. Named for the trouserlike undergarments that had recently liberated women to move more freely, these teams quickly established that they were anything but dainty with a string of decisive wins over male competition. In fact, they were so good that men such as the future Hall of Famer Rogers Hornsby occasionally asked to play with them to sharpen their skills.

Change was clearly in the air. Once women demonstrated that they could handle the physical and psychological stress of competition, there was no going back. Cultural barriers remained, however, and these could be formidable. Reconciling the traditional image of the passive, fragile woman with her new incarnation as an athlete proved a major challenge. In 1893, at the World's Congress of Representative Women in Chicago, Mrs. Minna Gordon Gould, a teacher of elocution with a keen interest in "physical culture," gave an address titled "Harmonious Adjustment Through Exercise." It expressed her era's shifting view of the value of sports for women, while also demonstrating the balancing act late Victorian women were often forced to perform if they were to engage in athletic activities while still remaining within the bounds of propriety.

Gould's speech started out in a thoroughly conventional vein, stating that "the wish all women have to be beautiful seems to me as natural as for birds to sing or for flowers to exhale perfume." She then went on to claim that a "beautiful body is one which is harmoniously developed in all its parts, whose organs are formed as nature intended, and which perform their functions according to nature's laws. Any deviation from this standard is deformity." This was followed by the assertion that deformity could be especially egregious in "the case of athletes, who often injure their health by undue exercise of some muscles of the body at the expense and neglect of others, especially in failing to maintain the balance between the organs that supply and those that waste the vital force."

Notice the dexterity of Gould's argument. While claiming that women wanted to be beautiful and warning against overindulgence in athletic activity, she also advocated against standards of health and beauty that would confine women to the parlor and the fainting couch. Gould was particularly incensed by corsets, railing against the "abnormal development in the fashionable woman, who compresses her waist by means of corsets," whose effect on the female figure she called "inartistic."

After setting the parameters of her view of a woman's proper health, Gould then proposed a regimen in which women did not fight against the bodies they were given with diet regimens, drugs, constricting clothes, or obsessive exercise, but rather celebrated their natural figures through a program of rigorous walking. "It is motion that gives value to exercise, and not the straining of the muscles by gymnastic appliances of heavy dumb-bells and Indian clubs, etc. The less apparatus one uses in exercise the better." With Gould and thinkers like her, beauty came to be associated with unadorned good health maintained by regular exercise. It may not have been Martina Navratilova, but it was also not the static, consumptive Pre-Raphaelite ideal of beauty, either.

This view of the active woman was bolstered by the groundbreaking work of the Stanford-educated physician Clelia Duel Mosher. Born in 1863, Mosher established in a groundbreaking master's thesis that the prevailing viewpoint that women breathed from the chest, and therefore took in less oxygen than men who breathed from the diaphragm, was simply wrong. Both sexes employed the same method of breathing. The reason for the discrepancy, Mosher discovered, was that in the past women had been tested while wearing diaphragm-constricting corsets. Though her work was slow to take hold, it inspired generations of researchers, coaches, and trainers to start looking at what women could do on the playing field, rather than what they could not.

Once women started walking, it would not be long until they began running. The female athlete was not only plausible. She was inevitable. The quickest avenue toward this liberation was the Olympics. Unfortunately, the driving force behind the Olympic movement was even less receptive to women than he was to athletes of color. In 1902, Coubertin declared that sports for women were "against the laws of nature." He stated that their participation in his games would be "*impratique, inintéressante, inesthétique et incorrecte*"—impractical, uninteresting, unsightly, and wrong. Coubertin was not alone. In 1894, the muckraking journalist H. L. Mencken wrote that "if I had my way . . . all female athletes would be shipped to the white-slave corrals of the Argentine."

Despite such protests, there was ultimately nothing that chauvinistic men and their female sympathizers could do to stop women from taking the field. Although women were not officially allowed to compete until the second Olympics in 1900, one did try to participate at the inaugural Athens Games in 1896. Stamata Revithi, a poor Greek who had recently lost one of her two children, attempted to enter the marathon, only to be turned away by officials. Undaunted, she ran the course on her own the next day. Her time may have been slow, but she finished. Some reporters called her Melpomene, after the Greek muse of tragedy. It was a nicely poetic touch that conveniently obscured the fact that they were too indifferent to learn her actual name.

Over the next few decades, women's participation in the Olympics saw steady if uneven progress. Croquet and ballooning were among the earliest sports in which females were allowed to compete. Women's gymnastics, meanwhile, was not recognized as an official event until Amsterdam in 1928. Neither was track and field, which then had an inauspicious beginning. In the 800 meters, so many women "collapsed" at the end of the 1928 finals that authorities banned the event until 1960, while the 1500 meters would not be run until 1972. Not surprisingly, no such prohibition for the opposite sex followed the near death of Dorando Pietri, who famously had to be dragged across the finish line of the men's marathon in 1908.

Despite steady progress and occasional great strides, women athletes remained deeply problematical figures through much of the 20th century. Every advance seemed to come with an asterisk intended to remind the world that females were not true athletes. For instance, women may have been allowed to compete in track and field at the 1928 Olympics, but they were also told that their shorts could not rise higher than 4 inches above the knee. Sometimes this belief that women were too fragile to compete at the same level as men masked the same sort of self-protective impulses as white establishment bans against blacks. Losing to a black guy may have been humiliating, but losing to a *girl* was unthinkable.

This thinking was probably at work in the case with the baseball pitcher Virne "Jackie" Mitchell, a 17-year-old Tennessee fireballer who was so good that a minor league men's team, the Chattanooga Lookouts, offered her a contract in 1931. Soon afterward, she struck out both Babe Ruth and Lou Gehrig in an exhibition game. Just days later, baseball commissioner Judge Kenesaw Mountain Landis, who vies with Avery Brundage as the most reactionary figure in the history of American sports, canceled Mitchell's contract and banned all women from professional baseball. As with Landis's prohibition on blacks, his bigotry eventually led to the formation of a separate league. Founded in 1943, the All-American Girls Professional Baseball League was able to draw large crowds to minor league baseball stadiums that had been left largely empty when male players had gone off to serve in World War II. Formed by the legendary Chicago Cubs owner and chewing-gum magnate Philip Wrigley, the league initially banned overhand pitching, though by 1945 the women were allowed to throw heat in exactly the same way as their male counterparts. Many of the teams were based in upper Midwestern centers of war production such as Racine, Wisconsin, and South Bend, Indiana, where other women also crossed the sexual divide by taking jobs in factories making weaponry and heavy machinery. By most accounts, the action was often as skilled and intense as anything performed by the minor leaguers the women were replacing.

The balancing act between competitive urges and ladylike decorum remained a difficult one, even for some of the era's foremost female athletes. The case of Eleanor Holm illustrates this burden. After winning the gold medal in the 100-meter backstroke in 1932 Olympics in Los Angeles, the eminently photogenic teenager was immediately courted by nearby Hollywood studios. She soon married the big band leader Art Jarrett. Although she had initially retired from the sport to pursue her film career, she decided to give swimming one more try for the 1936 Berlin Games. From the first, her disregard for the puritanical guidelines of Brundage's Olympic Committee got her into hot water. When asked by a journalist how she prepared for races, Holm breezily replied "with plenty of champagne and not much training." Matters finally came to a head on the boat trip to Berlin, where Holm's chaperone, the primly named Ada Y. Sackett, reported that the swimmer had been up drinking all night with a group of friends that included the actress Helen Hayes. After being discovered by officials in her room "in a deep slumber which approached a state of coma," Holm was kicked off the team by Brundage, even though it was well known that male Olympians on the boat had also broken training by getting drunk. Although Holm's behavior shocked the male establishment, at least no one questioned her femininity. She would go on to play opposite fellow Olympian Glenn Morris's man of the jungle in the 1938 *Tarzan's Revenge*, then star with fellow champion swimmer Johnny Weissmuller in a popular live aquatic show. Many leading female athletes of the era were not so easily accepted. Texas-born

Babe Didrikson is now seen as the greatest female athlete of her time, perhaps of all time. Like Lottie Dod, she excelled in any sport she attempted. After winning six of the ten track and field events on offer at the 1932 AAU Championships, she won two golds in the Olympic Games later that year, and would have won a third if officials had not mistakenly deemed her high-jumping style illegal. She then went on to become one of the greatest golfers of all time. And yet she was also the target of a constant torrent of abuse in which her femininity was ruthlessly questioned. The sportswriter Paul Gallico nicknamed the lean, short-haired athlete "Muscle Moll." He even derided her for sweating. At first Didrikson was defiant. When asked if there was any game she did not play, she answered, "Yeah, dolls." Deep down, however, the abuse rankled. Her decision to take up golf, a sport Gallico and his ilk considered at least marginally ladylike, is widely believed to have stemmed from her fatigue at the ongoing criticism.

The central subtext to these criticisms was the belief that most female athletes were lesbians. At times, however, the issue became gender itself. This anxiety first came into the public spotlight in 1936, when questions arose as to the sexual identity of two sprinters, Helen Stephens and Stella Walsh. Walsh, who was born Stanislawa Walasiewicz in Poland but grew up in Ohio using her Americanized name, wound up running for her country of birth in the 1932 Los Angeles Olympics after American officials disqualified her for taking appearance payments from meet promoters. She won the gold medal in the 100-meter dash and, in 1936, once again running for Poland, she entered the games as a favorite to retain her title as the world's fastest woman. To the shock of many, she was beaten by the American Stephens. Some Polish officials, claiming that no woman on earth could have beaten their star, accused Stephens of being male. She was subjected to a visual "sex test" by doctors, who affirmed that she was indeed female. No one thought to test Walsh, which was fortunate for her, because forty four years later, after she was murdered during a robbery in Cleveland, it was discovered during the autopsy that she had a tiny penis and testes. Perhaps inevitably, she became known forever after as "Stella the Fella."

Even though Walsh's secret remained undiscovered, concern about female athletes with male sexual characteristics, particularly testosterone-producing testes, became part of sports. Often, these suspicions were used by bigots to intimidate or denigrate female competitors. In the 1940s, the racist Olympic official Norman Cox infamously suggested that a special category of competition, "unfairly advantaged 'hermaphrodites,'" should be established for black women athletes. In Cox's view "normal women," whom he also described as a "childbearing," were hampered by "largish breasts, wide hips and knocked knees," liabilities women of African descent supposedly did not share. Evidence that Cox was not alone in his biases emerged in the following decade, when the black champion tennis player Althea Gibson was forced in 1957 to take a test to see if she had an extra chromosome. The belief that female athletes, especially African American ones, deviate in some way from the feminine ideal continues to hold sway with a significant strata of society, as the widely popular radio host Don Imus proved with his 2007 remark that the black players on Rutgers University's women's basketball team looked like "nappy-headed hos." The depth of public outrage over Imus's comments was reflected by the length of his suspension from his radio network—two weeks.

Against this backdrop of racist-fueled sexism, the achievements of pioneering black women athletes like Gibson become all the more remarkable. Perhaps the greatest trailblazer of them all was the sprinter Wilma Rudolph. One of twenty children in a poor but tightly knit Tennessee family, Rudolph was only four and a half pounds at birth. At the age of 4, she contracted polio, causing her to lose the use of her left leg. As a course of therapy, family members would take turns massaging her paralyzed limb. Some days she would receive as many as 10 massages from brothers and sisters. After five years in a leg brace, the iron-willed Rudolph was finally able to walk unencumbered. She quickly set about making up for lost time. Soon she was beating the boys in her neighborhood at basketball, a sport at which she excelled in high school. It was at school that she also discovered track and field. She made such great strides that she was able to bring back a bronze medal in the 4 x 100 relay from the 1956 Melbourne Olympics. Four years later, she buried the competition to win three gold medals at the 1960 Rome Games, running with a style so graceful French sportswriters called her "La Gazelle Noire."

Questions of gender identity are not always cover for racial prejudice or sexism. In the 1960s, the Soviet sisters Tamara and Irina Press became the subject of a controversy considerably more justified than the aspersions cast on Didrikson, Stephens, and Gibson. In the 1960 Rome Games, Irina finished first in the 80-meter hurdles, while her sister won a gold in the shot put and a silver in the discus. Four years later, Irina won the gold in the inaugural pentathlon, while Tamara this time took first place in both of her events. As their accomplishments piled up, questions began to be raised. Many believed that the sisters were simply too big and too strong to be women, especially when compared to their competitors. In response, the International Association of Athletics Federations (IAAF) instituted gender tests for international competitors in 1966. Despite being at the top of their games, both women immediately retired from competition and were therefore never tested. Their nicknames became the Press Brothers.

Despite this highly publicized start, both the International Olympic Committee (IOC) and the IAAF had stopped compulsory chromosome testing by 1999. The reason was simple: No one was able to come up with a universally accepted way of establishing what differentiated one sex from another. Scientific and cultural advances had blurred the line between male and female. There was no longer a single test, a sole criterion, that could be applied to settle the matter. The problems with sex testing were highlighted at the 1996 Atlanta Olympics, when eight female athletes tested positive for the SRY gene, which triggers growth of testes in a fetus. Under the old guidelines, this would have constituted prima facie evidence that all of these athletes were gendered male. And yet all eight were subsequently found to have conditions that caused a "false positive" for this test, giving them no competitive advantage. Since then, the entire notion of what constitutes a "female" athlete has been in a state of flux.

The case of Caster Semenya illustrates this complexity. The South African middle-distance runner exploded onto the international track scene as an 18-year-old in 2009, lowering her personal best in the 800 meters by seven seconds en route to a victory in the World Championships. Given the magnitude of her improvement in such a short period of time, as well as considerable comment about her muscular appearance, charges were leveled that she was either a hermaphrodite or using male hormones. Authorities at the IAAF ordered her to undergo a gender test after the organization's head, Pierre Weiss, pointedly remarked that "it is clear that she is a woman but maybe not 100 percent." In other words, the issue was not if Semenya was male, but rather if she was entirely female. Further complicating matters were suggestions that there was a racial element to the suspicions, with the runner being subjected to the same prejudice that Althea Gibson and other athletes of African descent had suffered. The testing protocol used on Semenya proved extensive, involving an endocrinologist, a gynecologist, an internal medicine specialist, an "expert on gender," and a psychologist. It took a year for her to be cleared to compete as a female athlete. Although detailed results of the test are kept secret for privacy reasons, rumors continued to swirl around the runner as she struggled to retain her old form after a year's exile from competition.

As compelling as discussions of gender could be, the issue of femininity became less of an obstacle to most girls and women as the 20th century advanced. They simply wanted the chance to play. Even as the culture grew less hostile toward the prospect of the female athlete, the field of play remained decidedly tilted in favor of males. On just about every level, from youth leagues through college athletics right on up to the professional ranks, women remained second-class citizens. And the men, acting like a rec league baseball team that hogs the neighborhood diamond, showed no sign that they meant to relinquish the field any time soon.

The first sustained attempt to deal with this inequity came in 1972, when several hundred mostly male, mostly out-of-shape United States congressmen passed a piece of legislation that would come to be known simply as Title IX. It turned out to be one of the most influential moments in the development of the woman athlete. It stated that "no person in the United States shall, on the basis of sex, be excluded from participation in, be denied the benefits of, or be subjected to discrimination under any education program or activity receiving Federal financial assistance." In other words, the female athlete was no longer a second-class citizen, at least not in the eyes of the United States government. Enacted three years later, the law meant that every institution that relied on federal funding had to provide equal playing fields for boys and girls. Cramped locker rooms, hand-me-down uniforms, and a limited selection of sports would no longer be acceptable. Teams might still be separate, but they would now have to be equal.

The beneficial effects among young female athletes were immediate. In 1970, roughly 294,000 American high school girls took part in high school sports. By 1973, before the law had even begun to be officially enforced, there were 1.3 million girls participating. In 1974, after Maria Pepe of Hoboken, New Jersey, won her suit against Little League Baseball for being dropped from her team because of her sex, one of America's most sacred sporting institutions was compelled to admit girls. A young player named Bunny Taylor proved the wisdom of the decision when she almost immediately became the first girl to throw a no-hitter. In 1976, basketball player Ann Meyers, who was a high school freshman when Title IX was passed, became the first female recipient of a full athletic scholarship at UCLA, the greatest collegiate basketball program in the history of that sport.

Although the effects of Title IX would take a generation to begin to reach the professional level, passage of the act seemed to galvanize women athletes across the spectrum from the first day. Suddenly, disguises like those used by Kathryn "Tubby" Johnston, who in 1950 played Little League masquerading as a boy, or Kathrine Switzer, who entered the 1967 Boston Marathon as "K. Switzer" and was only able to keep her number after her boyfriend body-blocked an official trying to stop her, were no longer required. Athletes like hot rod driver Shirley Muldowney and jockey Diane Crump competed in sports that were formerly all-male preserves. Big business did not hesitate to take advantage of this new market. The manufacture of specialized sportswear and equipment for women athletes skyrocketed through the 1970s. More controversially, the Philip Morris tobacco company, whose women-oriented Virginia Slims cigarette was promoted by the slogan "You've come a long way, baby," cashed in on this boom by becoming the chief sponsor of the Women's Tennis Association Tour.

Even in traditionally "feminine" sports, a newly competitive spirit was on display. Sports like gymnastics, figure skating, and tennis, once considered proper female domains because of their gentility, soon became characterized by power and aggression that matched anything the boys could offer. Competitors like tennis champion Martina Navratilova simply did not accept the fact that they had to play the game more gently than men. Nowhere was this new athleticism more clear than in the performance of the great Russian gymnast Ludmilla Tourischeva at the 1975 World Championships in London. At the moment she dismounted from the uneven bars, the apparatus suffered a complete collapse behind her as she flew through the air to her landing. Her routine finished,

Tourischeva, in a remarkable display of steely nerves, walked from the mat without so much as a backward glance, as if wrecking equipment was something she did regularly. Nobody had to provide her with a shoulder to cry on. When asked about her performance, her trainer Vladislav Rastorotsky remarked, "Ludmilla would fight to the death in any situation."

One of most visible events involving a female athlete during the Title IX era combined history, competition, and spectacle in a uniquely American manner. In September 1973, Billie Jean King, one of the world's top-rated women's tennis players, met 55-year-old Bobby Riggs in a televised match inevitably dubbed "The Battle of the Sexes." Riggs, a former Wimbledon champion who had defeated Margaret Court on Mother's Day in a similar showdown earlier that year, brashly declared that a victory over King, a passionate proponent of women's rights, would establish the superiority of the male athlete. The atmosphere at the Houston Astrodome was carnival-like, with Riggs entering the stadium in a carriage pulled by women, while King arrived on a litter carried by strapping young men in togas. But once the game started, both players proved themselves to be deadly serious. King easily beat Riggs in straight sets. No one believed the match proved anything important about the difference between the sexes. King would have needed to beat a top-rated player like Ilie Nastase or Jimmy Connors to do that. The spectacle, however, did suggest that there could now come a day when men and women would face each other across the net on an equal footing in the course of a normal tournament.

There was a dark side to this new sense of female empowerment. During the time that Title IX was taking hold in the United

States, the East German communist government was also taking action to help its own female athletes. Their approach, however, was considerably more forthright. Beginning in 1974, it became official policy of the powerful East German Sports Performance Committee to systematically dope nearly all of the nation's top athletes. Although competitors of both sexes were "treated," it was women who were most deeply affected by a regimen based on Oral-Turinabol, an anabolic steroid that boosted the recipient's testosterone level. Girls as young as 12 were put on the program, though athletes were only ever informed that they were being given "vitamins." Informers for the Stasi, the feared state security apparatus, would immediately report on any athlete who questioned the exact chemical nature of the "blue bean," as the Oral-Turinabol pill came to be known.

The results were immediate and dramatic, nowhere more evident than in the performance of the DDR women's swim team in the 1976 Montreal Olympics. Led by the formidable Kornelia Ender, female East German swimmers won eleven of the thirteen events contested. Ender, who had gained eighteen pounds of pure muscle in the months leading up to the games, won all four races in which she competed, each in world-record time. It was not for another ten years, when steroid use became more common in the West, that effective tests were established to detect them. Even then, the East German authorities were able to plant a mole on the international regulatory board who was able to advise scientists back home about the nature of the tests. East German women remained virtually unbeatable.

The fallout from these experiments was severe. Among these women athletes, side effects ranged from abnormal hair growth and deepened voices to infertility and breast cancer. One of the more extreme cases involved the European champion shot-putter Heidi Krieger. Subjected to the same regimen as her swimming compatriots, she eventually developed strongly male characteristics. In 1997, she underwent sexual reassignment surgery and is now known as Andreas Krieger.

By the 1980s, the image of the female athlete had undergone a radical transformation. True, there were still fans, commentators, and even some male athletes who thought of her as second class or even freakish. But these figures were now seen to be reactionary buffoons. This is not to say that Title IX has turned out to be a complete panacea. At Division I colleges, for example, athletic directors often have to perform strenuous statistical gymnastics to make it seem women's sports are on an equal footing with men's programs, especially football teams that can have up to a hundred members and fly to nationally broadcast games on charter jets. But on a grassroots level, there is no disputing that equality is now the norm. In sports like soccer, the rate of new female players far outstrips that of males, while girls are beginning to play traditionally "boy" sports like lacrosse and rugby in ever-increasing numbers.

While professional sports have by and large not yet reached anything that could be called equity, leagues like the WNBA and Women's Professional Soccer have also made tremendous strides in the last few decades. Professional women tennis players may still play fewer sets for less prize money than their male counterparts, but anyone who has witnessed a 127-mile-per-hour serve from Venus Williams knows that those days surely must be numbered.

Perhaps even more important than accomplishments measured by playing statistics or attendance figures are the strides women athletes have made in capturing the imagination of an increasingly broad base of fans. Although we can admire the achievements of Lottie Dod, Babe Didrikson, and Wilma Rudolph, no one for a moment can pretend that these women possessed an iconic power on a level with their contemporaries John L. Sullivan, Babe Ruth, or Mickey Mantle. The chance of a young girl idolizing the female Babe was far less than her brother dreaming about being the male one.

That situation is clearly changing. One can see it most readily in how big businesses spend their marketing dollars. Fifty years ago, there was very little demand for women athletes to do endorsement deals. By 1996, Sheryl Swoopes had become the first woman basketball player to have a shoe named after her. Made by Nike, it was called "Air Swoopes" in reference to the company's best-selling "Air Jordan." Now, top athletes like Maria Sharapova and Indy-car driver Danica Patrick can command multimillion-dollar advertising contracts that are gradually closing the gap with their male counterparts. While these campaigns may still be dependent on how telegenic the subject may be, it is a long way from the virtual invisibility of just a few decades ago.

The woman athlete's ability to grip the public imagination can run far deeper than simply selling merchandise, as Brandi Chastain and her teammates showed at the World Cup. Their victory fired the imaginations of a generation of American girls who were just beginning to find their strength on thousands of soccer fields across the country. While it is difficult to measure the electrifying effect that the Algerian middle-distance runner Hassiba Boul-merka, 1500-meter gold medalist at the 1992 Olympics, must have had on other young female athletes from the Islamic world, there is no doubting her bravery for continuing to compete after her nation's fearsome Islamic Salvation Front condemned her for "running with naked legs in front of thousands of men."

The most dramatic example of the female athlete achieving an iconic status every bit as powerful as that of her male counterpart came in the 2000 Sydney Olympics. In the finals of the women's 400-meter dash, the clear favorite was Cathy Freeman, an Australian of Aboriginal descent. Although she was the two-time reigning world champion, Freeman's position as the emotional epicenter for the hometown crowd came from a source much more profound than the chance of a rare Australian track and field medal. Because of her ethnicity, Freeman had become a symbol of reconciliation for a nation with a long history of discrimination against its indigenous population. By running to victory, she would help symbolically deliver her people from years of oppression. By cheering her on in the stadium, white Australians would ritually ask forgiveness for their past sins.

As Freeman came to the starting line in a sleek hooded body suit, her face bore the strain of expectation. And yet it also showed the sort of determination and strength that had been present in the often unnamed female athletes who competed in second-class games since antiquity. Although the race remained close as Freeman entered the home stretch, she began to pull away in the final 50 meters, as if the thunderous cheers of the home crowd were adding a few inches to her every stride. She won big, setting off a raucous celebration every bit equal to that Spyridon Louis had ignited a century earlier when he conjured national joy by the mere act of running. Among the outpouring of commentary that followed her victory, much was said about racism and reconciliation in Australia, and the athlete's ability to bring people together. Considerably less was said about the fact that the athlete who had accomplished this was female. Which, after 3,000 years of struggle, may have been the day's greatest victory of all.

CHAPTER 10

UP CLOSE AND PERSONAL

At the 1992 Olympic Games in Barcelona, the United States fielded what was undoubtedly the greatest basketball team in the history of the sport. Featuring legends Michael Jordan, Magic Johnson, and Larry Bird, the "Dream Team" easily went undefeated en route to capturing the gold medal. During most of their games, they played with a sort of youthful abandon, as if the Olympic tournament was nothing more than an exhibition for their unparalleled skills. Players from opposing teams would sometimes seem transfixed by the frolicking Americans during games. On those rare occasions the other side would begin to threaten the Dream Team, Jordan and company would abandon their acrobatic dunks and trick passes for serious play. Dominance was quickly reestablished; the USA truly was invincible.

The only discordant note came during the medal ceremony, when Jordan staged a silent protest amid the general exultation. Unlike Tommie Smith and John Carlos twenty four years earlier, his gesture had nothing to do with politics. He was not speaking out against racism, poverty, or war. Rather, he was objecting to his sweat suit—specifically, to the fact that the USOC was forcing him to wear one manufactured by Reebok. Jordan, of course, was a Nike man, *the* Nike man, with his own line of shoes and clothing featuring the famous "Jumpman" logo. It was a relationship that could earn the Chicago Bulls star upward of $1 billion before the last Air Jordan sneaker is sold.

Juggling his allegiances with a dexterity that rivaled his ball-handling skills, Jordan got hold of an American flag before the medal ceremony and artfully draped it over his shoulder to cover the offending logo, like some prudish church official covering the naughty bits of a classical sculpture. While his black predecessors may have played for two teams, one denoted by the name on their uniform and the other by the color of their skin, Jordan now played for a third outfit as well. Its flag bore the Nike swoosh symbol.

Jordan's actions demonstrated just what a powerful nexus of symbols the athlete has become. Never in history has he meant so many different things to so many different people. Some of these symbols contradict one another; others are complementary. Some involve marketing strategies and mass consumption; others represent more intangible qualities like courage, ethnic pride, patriotism, and rage. And it is not just Jordan who represents so many different interests. Each of the top stars on the medal stand at the Pavelló Olímpic de Badalona in 1992 radiated a dizzying array of meanings. In addition to Nike, Jordan signified Chicago, Coke, and black America; Bird stood for Boston, Converse shoes, Miller Lite beer, and the ever-shrinking white representation on the professional basketball court. Johnson, in addition to his own corporate and civic associations, had added another entry to his suite of signifiers—the previous year, he had publicly announced that he was HIV positive. And of course, as the echoing chants of "USA!" and those red, white, and blue flags throughout the arena confirmed, all three men represented the United States of America.

The Dream Team, whose very name suggests something that transcends the everyday, marked the culmination of a process that had been going on since people began gathering in that flyblown corner of Greece almost 3,000 years earlier. The athlete has captured the Western imagination and, indeed, that of much of the world. A top athlete now exercises unprecedented power in both the global economy and the fantasy lives of his public. Liberated from long-term relationships to teams, cities, and even nations, he has now taken unprecedented control of his public personae. No one rivals him. Not movie stars, not politicians, not religious leaders. However popular such figures might be, their power is bounded by taste, borders, or tradition. The athlete has no such restrictions. When he is at the top of his game and his fame, he is truly a free agent.

More than a decade after his retirement, Jordan remains the prime example of this supremacy. From the moment he turned professional, he understood the potential power of his image and demonstrated his intent to manage it as closely as possible. Aided by a farsighted agent, David Falk, and a visionary coach, Phil Jackson, Jordan made all the right moves, on the court and off. His relationship with Nike, under the direction of a brilliant ad man, Jim Riswold of Wieden+Kennedy, has proven the most fertile in the history of sports sponsorship. But it was only one part of the equation. As the scholar Henry Louis Gates has noted, Jordan not only enhanced the Nike brand, it enhanced him. Riswold's groundbreaking Air Jordan campaign may have sold warehouses full of merchandise, but it also magnified Jordan's image in the public mind, allowing him to sign ever-more-lucrative deals with other companies. It made him a household presence. Jordan no longer just represented a brand. He was one.

Other leading athletes now operate in the world Michael built. The competitor is responsible not just for scoring points but also for managing his public image. Decisions about where and even how to play are based not only upon salary but also on which franchise will best fuel an athlete's iconic power. An all-star base-ball player's desire to be traded from Kansas City or Milwaukee to New York or Los Angeles is motivated at least in part by the pros-pect of playing in a bigger media market. When LeBron James decided to leave gritty Cleveland for glittering Miami, he made it clear that his only loyalty was to himself. "I wanted to do what was best for LeBron James and make him happy," explained the man with "CHOSEN1" tattooed across his broad back. His shift from first person to third within the space of a single sentence suggests that this was an athlete wholly comfortable with think-ing of himself as a brand. Equally revealing was the fact that James identified his new destination as "South Beach," home of pop stars, mansions, and night clubs but not, it turns out, the Miami Heat, who played in an arena located in plain old downtown Miami.

The phenomenon of athletic autonomy is not limited only to leading professionals. While college athletes are still largely bound by NCAA guidelines and professional drafts, the behavior of those short-listed for the Heisman Trophy can often resemble that of actors chasing Academy Awards. The process of self-promotion now begins earlier and earlier. It is not unusual for top high school football or basketball prospects to mount campaigns during the recruiting process that include slickly produced highlight reels. The very best players may even hold press conferences on National Signing Day to announce the school they have chosen. Where a local hero from Wichita was once torn between the University of Kansas, Kansas State, and maybe, just maybe, the University of Oklahoma, he will now scour all fifty states for the program that best fits his needs. And it does not end there: the families of junior high and even elementary school prodigies will often decide where to live based upon the quality of the local high school's teams. The process reached a new level of absurdity in early 2010 when Lane Kiffin, the head coach of the University of Southern California Trojan football team, announced that he had accepted a verbal commitment from a 13-year-old prospect from Delaware.

Young athletes no longer feel compelled to perform in their native countries. Prodigies from Ireland to China will go to great lengths to attend universities in the United States to enhance their chances of getting noticed by professional scouts. Those who are not yet old enough for college can attend year-round academies like the one run by the IMG sports agency in Florida, which offers intensive training and high school diplomas to up-and-coming tennis and basketball players from nearly every precinct of the planet.

Professional athletes on nearly every continent are also liberating themselves from traditional structures and institutions. Although some adventurous South American soccer players were offering their services to European clubs as early as the 1930s, it was not until 1995, when Jean-Marc Bosman challenged the rigid system that tied him indefinitely to his Belgian club, that European soccer players became free to move from one team to another.

Just as important, the same European Court of Justice ruling allowed clubs that had previously been limited to a small number of foreign players to fill their rosters in any way they chose. Teams like Chelsea and Real Madrid, once composed almost entirely of talent from the home country, have since become transnational entities, dream teams in their own right. Merchandising and satellite broadcasting ensure that anyone can be a fan. Brand name players like David Beckham and Cristiano Ronaldo can now move in a stratosphere where the only constraint on a player is the lucrative, usually short-term contract he signed.

The free movement of athletes has also changed the face of America's pastime, now as globalized as European soccer. Baseball players from Japan, Korea, and especially Latin America are common at American ballparks. Although the Dominican Republic has a population of only around 10 million, it has proved a particularly fertile source for Major League players. Japan's Ichiro Suzuki, the all-star right fielder for the Seattle Mariners, is a prime example of the new globalized athlete. He began his career in his native country, where baseball was introduced by American missionaries in the 1870s and remained popular even during World War II. After nine seasons dominating Japanese baseball, Ichiro moved seamlessly into the American game in 2001, where he became instantly popular with the Seattle fans, a fair portion of whom were of Japanese ancestry. He also remained famous in his native land. Neither nation has the right to call him their own, any more than Seattle does when his current contract expires. Ichiro will be Ichiro wherever he picks up a bat. Even his batting style is multicultural, his samurai-like batting ritual giving way to the pure swing of a Ty Cobb or Ted Williams the moment the ball approaches the plate.

This global mobility has created athletes of ever more potent charisma. Observing the laws of physics, their auras lose no energy by transferring from one state to another. Electronic media further magnify the athlete's image, powering it right into the core of the spectator's brain. Television and the internet allow him to be everywhere at once. A great goal or clutch shot can be plucked out of the flow of time and inserted into an infinite loop, and every repeated showing generates a little more heat. It took the foremost Greek poets and historians to perpetuate the performances of Leonidas of Rhodes and Milo of Croton; now YouTube can immortalize an extraordinary performance before a game has even ended.

This omnipresence has done more than allow the athlete to bag bigger contracts or become a more effective salesman. It has also implicated him even more deeply in the emotional lives of many spectators, who come to feel as if they have a right to participate in his private life. They are invested in his struggles and redemptions off the field as well as on it. In his own day, Lou Gehrig's terse statement that he had been given a "bad break" was deemed sufficient to describe the sudden onset of a terrifying disease. Now he would be expected to appear at a press conference, backlit by MRIs and flanked by a team of neurologists. The public would demand to be told his prognosis and course of treatment. More than anything, they would want to *know how it felt*. Not just to win or lose, but also to experience the triumphs and trials of daily life. When Joe DiMaggio's marriage to Marilyn Monroe ended after only 274 days, the actress cited "mental cruelty" as the grounds for divorce, without further elaboration. Anyone who believes that would be the end of the story these days is simply not paying attention.

It is not just about gossip. There is a moral dimension to this presumed intimacy. Athletes are now supposed to inspire us with more than just their play. While the competitor's performance has been used as a source of uplift since the dying wrestler Arrichion refused to give up the fight, his entire life is now expected to be exemplary. People who once only expected the athlete to play with courage and skill now look to him for guidance in matters that have nothing to do with scoring goals or hitting home runs. Although he has occasionally risen to this challenge, these great expectations have mostly led to an increasingly profound sense of disillusionment.

Modern image architects have responded to this hunger for an exemplary athlete by creating sophisticated myths about him. Filmmakers have led the way. This is not surprising. Athletes seem to have been purposefully designed for the big screen. They define themselves through action, they are generally young and often attractive, and their dramas climax in the dramatic set pieces of big games. They even wear different-colored uniforms so you can tell the good guys from the bad.

From the first, movies relocated the athlete's struggles from the field of play to a nonsporting location. More often than not, this new arena was the hospital bed. *The Pride of the Yankees* (1942) told Gehrig's sad story, while *Knute Rockne All American* (1940) depicted the Notre Dame football player George Gipp, whose early death proved inspirational to his teammates and gave birth to the immortal line "Win one for the Gipper!" In both movies, disease becomes an opponent that provides the hero with the chance to become a model of courage and stoicism. As his uniform becomes a hospital gown, his forbearance proves a lesson for us all.

Despite the advent of the film antihero in the late 1960s, the screen athlete remained stubbornly inspirational. In *Bang the Drum Slowly* (1973), a naive young baseball catcher contracts a fatal blood disease; in *Brian's Song* (1971), the real-life Chicago Bears fullback Brian Piccolo is forced to combat cancer. Even when films take a more cynical turn, the athlete can remain an inspirational figure. In the black comedy *North Dallas Forty* (1979), football players are depicted as hard-drinking, pill-popping, philandering gladiators who are forced to deal with chronic injuries and an exploitative management. The movie's hero, Phillip Elliott (played by Nick Nolte), nevertheless manages to maintain his dignity even as he makes compromises with a system he cannot defeat. And then there is the Academy Award–winning *Rocky* (1976), in which integrity and hard work are rewarded not with a championship, but with personal redemption, universal respect, and the love of a good woman.

This mythmaking approach eventually came to inform how television producers and sportscasters depicted real-world athletes. Understanding that simply broadcasting an athlete's performances would not satisfy their rapidly expanding audience, sports television producers began to flesh him or her out, to give the actual competitor the same narrative arc as his film counterparts. ABC's groundbreaking *Wide World of Sports*, which debuted in 1961 and covered sports ranging from rattlesnake hunting to slow-pitch softball, explicitly stated in its famous opening narration that its mission was to bring us "the human drama of athletic competition." That show was produced by Roone Arledge, whose efforts to humanize the athlete would become even more pronounced during the 1972 Munich Olympics, when he introduced a segment called "Up Close and Personal." These consisted of two- to four-minute biographical sketches of an athlete that were broadcast moments before he or she competed. The idea was not so much to highlight a competitor's past achievements as to give the viewer an emotional context for experiencing the upcoming event. Although the first of these segments tended to be rather fluffy, such as one on the gardening habits of a Soviet superheavyweight weight lifter, before long they had become potent micro-dramas of behind-the-scenes struggle and deliverance. In 1984, one memorable piece on the US figure skater Elaine Zayak featured, in the words of veteran sportscaster Jim McKay, "the story behind the story." Accompanied by a sound track of heart-plucking piano music, the 18-year-old Zayak recounted how she began skating as therapy after losing two toes as a toddler in a lawn-mower accident. The segment ended with a close-up of the skater's mangled appendage, then segued into her live performance. It would take a flint-hearted spectator not to cheer her on. She went on to finish sixth. These days, athletes vie to be invited to visit the Connecticut studios of ESPN, not to sit down for an in-depth discussion of their career, but rather to record clever "This Is SportsCenter" promotional skits that make them look like good sports as well as good sportsmen.

In the race to capture the imagination of a spectator besieged by a mushrooming catalog of choices, it was often the athlete with the affecting backstory who won out. It did not matter if they were competing in an obscure sport that held little intrinsic interest for the viewer. Jeff Blatnick, an American Greco-Roman wrestler, became briefly famous when he won a gold medal in the 1984 Olympics after the audience was repeatedly informed that less than two years earlier he had his spleen and appendix removed while combating Hodgkin's lymphoma. Sixteen years after Blatnick, the same obscure sport made headlines when the Wyoming farm boy Rulon Gardner won the heavyweight gold after viewers were told all about his struggles with a childhood learning disability. Further upping the emotional stakes was the fact that his opponent was the apparently invincible Russian legend Alexander Karelin. Gardner's cartwheel after his victory became one of the most iconic moments of the 2000 Sydney Games, even though few Americans even understood the rules of the sport. He went on to battle his post-Olympic obesity on the popular reality show *The Biggest Loser*, a transition which seemed perfectly logical in the brave new world of sporting celebrity.

The cyclist Lance Armstrong provides the foremost modern example of the inspirational athlete. He is, first of all, one of the most gifted and successful competitors of his generation. His record of seven Tour de France wins is without equal. He is also a prodigiously hard worker who does everything in his power to enhance his natural gifts. At his peak, tests determined that his aerobic abilities were among the highest ever measured, roughly twice that of the average healthy adult male. He is also an outsider, a Texan in a sport usually dominated by Europeans.

None of this, however, would have been sufficient on its own to grant him truly iconic status. That came from his experience with cancer. In 1996, when the 25-year-old Armstrong was just coming into his own as a world-class cyclist, he was diagnosed with stage three testicular cancer. It soon spread to his lungs and brain. He was given a less than 50 percent chance of long-term survival. After an intensive course of chemotherapy, the disease was declared in remission two years later. To many, Armstrong was seen to have "beaten" cancer just as surely as he would defeat rivals on the steep roads of the Pyrenees. During this time, he founded the Lance Armstrong Foundation, a cancer-support charity whose Livestrong rubber bracelets adorn untold wrists worldwide. Without this narrative of victory over a fearsome disease, it is hard to see how an athlete toiling in a sport whose main dramas are played out in France could achieve such lasting fame in the United States.

The problem is, many leading athletes do not fit into this heroic mold. They cannot bear the iconic weight placed on them. In some cases, this is because they simply do not lead inspirational lives. Born with remarkable gifts, they are rewarded early by a culture that eases the way for them with college scholarships and epic signing bonuses. They work hard and play well, but once the final whistle blows, they face no greater adversary than fans who want autographs. Their statements on issues outside their expertise are bland. Their downtime is spent not doing charitable work or writing poetry, but unwinding from the stress of competition. All of which is perfectly understandable. They never signed on to be exemplars of morality or courage. They simply want to play.

In other cases, intense scrutiny leads to disenchantment. The athlete turns out to be selfish, petty, philandering, or substance abusing. Even if he remains heroic, his story might reveal truths about the world that that are anything but uplifting. Such is the case with Pat Tillman. A well-respected defensive back for the Arizona Cardinals, Tillman appeared to be the very model of the inspirational athlete when he famously turned his back on a lucrative new contract to join the US Army Rangers eight months after the attacks of 9/11. His free-flowing long hair was shaved off; his cardinal red uniform replaced with olive drab. After a brief burst of publicity, during which Tillman strengthened his image as a patriot by making no self-aggrandizing public statements, he disappeared from public view.

And then, nearly two years after his enlistment, news came that he had been killed during a firefight in Afghanistan. Politicians and military spokesman hailed him as a symbol of patriotic selflessness. Tillman's lantern-jawed image became omnipresent in the media, an icon in the war on terror. Before long, however, a very different picture emerged of the soldiering athlete and his death. It turned out that he had been killed by friendly fire, a fact officials had actively covered up in a conspiracy that probably went as high as Secretary of Defense Donald Rumsfeld. Not only that, but Tillman turned out to be a complicated figure, not the chiseled super-patriot the media portrayed, but rather a thoughtful young man who had been reading the radical left-wing philosopher Noam Chomsky and had come to believe that the Iraq War was wrong. His story remains a cautionary tale for those who believe athletes can be readily deployed as inspirational figures, especially in fields of endeavor outside of the stadium.

More often, it is the athlete and not the system who cracks under the strain of scrutiny and expectation. Even a figure as iconic as Armstrong is not immune from this process of disillusionment. In a sport with a long history of the use of performance-enhancing drugs, he has been the target of persistent doping allegations. Although he has been cleared by multiple tests, other riders have testified that they have seen him shooting up, allegations that appear ready to plague the Tour de France champion for the remainder of his life.

While Armstrong's good works largely indemnify him against these allegations, no such grace was extended to Tiger Woods, whose Icarus-like fall vividly illustrates the burden of iconic expectation. At first his career seemed to follow an arc every bit as inspirational as Armstrong's. One does not have to be a golfing fan to understand the magnitude of his accomplishments. He first rose to the top of the official world golf rankings in 1997, at the age of 21. Over the next thirteen years, he would spend a staggering 623 weeks in that position, including a run of 281 consecutive weeks. Both of these are records. During the same period he won fourteen major championships, an achievement second only to that of Jack Nicklaus. His win at the 1997 Masters is considered the greatest in the history of that tournament. If anything, his fifteen-stroke victory at the 2000 US Open in Pebble Beach was even more legendary. As was true with Armstrong, Woods's supremacy has been confirmed in a laboratory, where technicians using a stop-action camera originally designed for the Department of Defense timed Woods's swing at 120 miles per hour, some 15 miles per hour faster than the average among touring pros.

Added to these remarkable achievements was just the sort adversity that mythmakers crave: Woods was a black man in a sport that historically has not exactly been welcoming to players of color. A sense of what he had to contend with became very public just after Woods's first win at Augusta, when the white former champion Fuzzy Zoeller referred to him as "that little boy" and jokingly said that he should not serve "fried chicken . . . or collard greens or whatever the hell they serve" at the annual dinner traditionally hosted by the champion. Woods's response was an exemplary blend of righteous indignation and a willingness to forgive. Clearly, here was a young man who could serve as a model for anyone interested in making their way in a hostile environment.

But then Woods trashed the narrative. In 2009, after a car accident outside his Florida mansion while he was fleeing his enraged wife, it came to light that he had cheated with a number of women. The public outcry was intense. All those moments of sublime play and his battle against racism seemed to be immediately forgotten. Fans mocked him mercilessly. Tabloids published the content of his pornographic text messages. Fellow players in the notoriously polite golfing world publicly criticized him. Endorsement deals worth many millions of dollars were withdrawn. He was forced to make a humiliating public apology before entering a course of behavior modification at the Gentle Path rehab clinic. Just about the only thing he inspired now were cruel jokes by late-night talk-show hosts.

On the face of it, the reaction seemed all out of proportion. It was not as if the manufacturers of automobiles, wristwatches, or golf wear had initially asked him to endorse their products because he was an ideal husband. What, exactly, was his crime? In Woods's America, adultery is a recreational activity that might be even more popular than golf. He had not been caught flirting with spectators during tournaments; none of his lovers had blackmailed him to miss a crucial putt at Augusta as part of a gambling scheme. For over a decade, he had played with intensity, skill, and steely nerves, transforming a genteel country club game into a spectacle on par with the NBA or NFL. And he had done it in the face of subtle but enduring racism.

None of this mattered. He had broken a deeper contract, one he may have never really known he had made. By getting his jollies with cocktail waitresses, Woods had betrayed a public that had been taught that the ability to hit a three iron to within inches of a cup while millions watched translated into personal qualities like unflagging honesty and unadulterated devotion. Here was a man who had four times taken the winner's walk up the 18th fairway at Augusta, and now he had been discovered creeping around behind his wife's back. To many fans, the two images were irreconcilable. What compounded his sin was that he played a sport that was a bucolic fantasyland for largely affluent, socially conservative fans. And people did not only feel disappointment. Many reacted with the emotion that has become an important part of the public's relationship with the athlete. They hated him.

Of course, fans have always hated athletes. Brooklyn Dodgers fans hated players from the Giants, and the feeling was mutual. And both groups loathed the Yankees. In Scottish soccer, the animosity between Glasgow's Rangers and their crosstown rivals Celtic has been so intense for over a century that their "Old Firm" matches often seem like reenactments of the Battle of the Boyne. But this animosity was, in its own strange way, usually a product of devotion, even love. It was not personal. If the object of abuse happened to wear the jersey of the fan's home team a few seasons later, then all would be forgiven. Hate, of course, could also stem from racism or jingoism. Or it could come from cynics like Aristophanes and Thorstein Veblen, who simply had no time for sports. And, of course, there are those spasms of disgust directed at a fan's own player after a missed field goal, a third strike, a double fault. But these were no more than family squabbles, an argument among friends that would be dispelled as soon as the slump was broken.

But this new contempt for the athlete is something altogether different. It is existential. The hard fact is that many of the people who pay good money to sit in the stands or devote a hefty chunk of their day to watch an athlete on television do not like him one little bit, even if they wear a souvenir jersey with his name on it. He becomes a target for their frustrations with a disenchanting world. One need only visit the comments section of any website devoted to sports or hear the withering contempt of many callers on talk radio to understand that there is precious little adoration left for the icon.

One of the main reasons people hate the athlete is because he is seen to be greedy. The numbers tell the story: In 1951, Joe DiMaggio earned $100,000, while in 2010, one of his successors as Yankee star, Alex Rodriguez, made $32,000,000. In that same period, median household income in the United States rose from $3,515 to $50,221. And that was just Rodriguez's *salary*. When endorsement deals are also taken into consideration, some of the highest-paid sportsmen now make sums that the average fan can hardly comprehend.

In exchange for these stacks of cash, the athlete can be disloyal, selfish, and vain. Their followers suspect that they are probably juiced on performance-enhancing drugs on the field and recreational substances off it; that they cheat on their wives, beat their girlfriends, and spend more money in a strip club on a Saturday night than the average bleacher bum makes in a month. Or a year. And if enough of them do not get their way, they are more than capable of going on strike, robbing fans of a major source of distraction from increasingly difficult lives.

The new media transparency means that these transgressions not only can be laid bare by journalists but also can be reproduced relentlessly on Internet sites that have no real editor, no filter. If a well-known football player is caught sending a photograph of his genitalia to a woman as part of some crude courtship ritual, it is now likely that a 13-year-old boy who uses that star's official photograph as a screen saver on his computer will wind up seeing that image. It is doubtful that boy will grow up to view his hero as an exemplar of manly virtues, at least not the sort of manly virtues the mythmakers intended when they first started making the athlete the lead in America's morality plays.

But the fans still come. Game after game, season after season. They still gather in front of televisions to watch. They fill new stadiums paid for by their tax dollars, including a bond-funded $60 million *high school* stadium in Allen, Texas. They flocked to see Barry Bonds launch record-setting home runs into the San Francisco Bay, despite the widespread belief that he was using steroids. They watched the Florida Marlins after their infamous 2005 "market correction," in which profit-conscious owners effectively disbanded the team that had won the World Series two years earlier. They watched Mike Tyson after he had been jailed for rape and then had bitten off part of Evander Holyfield's ear. It can often seem as if there is nothing an athlete can do that will prevent people from making the effort necessary to follow him.

The main reason people still watch, of course, are the games themselves, which are available in ever-higher definition, in increasingly comfortable venues. Vast arrays of cameras render performances from classically heroic angles; JumboTrons immortalize great plays (or controversial ones) seconds after they happen.

Athletes are bigger, faster, and stronger than ever before. Seven-footers drain three-point shots with ease; 300-pound linemen move with the dexterity that players half their size once displayed. Globalization means that leagues that were formerly hermetically sealed have now been opened to vast new markets of talent. Soccer players from Ghana and Korea light up the English Premiership and Italy's Serie A; baseballers from Japan and the Caribbean provide some of the best talent in the major leagues. Basketball players from Croatia and Argentina, hockey players from Russia and Finland, golfers from South Africa and Taiwan—the energy they bring to the field of play helps fans overcome the bad taste left by the latest scandal. For four quarters or two halves or three periods, a game's mythic pull allows even the most censorious spectator to suspend disbelief. Franchises switch cities, and all this means is that a new wave of fans will click through the turnstiles. Strikes erase seasons, and the next year the stadiums fill, often with increased ticket prices. The athlete remains too important to be ruined by the mere mortals who inhabit his body.

There is a darker force behind this stubborn and apparently irrational loyalty. Some fans, or perhaps a part of every fan, enjoy the bad behavior. They get a kick out of discovering that there is some sinister power at work in the athletes whom they obsess over. People have always followed athletes for reasons that have little to do with finding role models or witnessing heroics. The *pankration,* the gladiatorial contests, the melee, bare-knuckle fighting, college football in its early days, mixed martial arts today—spectators have always wanted to see pain and blood and crushing defeat. They hunger for displays of anger and aggression. As a young Mike Tyson put it, "When you see me smash somebody's skull, you enjoy it."

Columnists, sportswriters, and television producers might want us to believe that the athlete brings out the best in us, but anyone attending a midseason New York Islanders game or a Millwall/West Ham match on a rainy Saturday in the East End of London will soon understand that there is more to the story. The difference now is that fans have come to expect, and perhaps secretly thrill, at violence and aggression that happens *off* the field of play. Homer celebrated the "shipwreck of chariots" at the funeral games for Patroclus. Spectators still like to see crashes, and if they sometimes happen in strip club VIP rooms or behind the wheel of leased Escalades, then that is just part of the game.

In his seminal 1966 work *On Aggression*, the Nobel Prize–winning zoologist Konrad Lorenz suggested that aggression was neither an aberration nor a curse, but rather an essential part of the evolution of most species. It is inherent, allowing us to survive in a hostile world. Problems arise only when it has no proper outlet. This has become especially true in modern man, whose civilization largely liberates him from the need for the regular displays of aggression his ancestors relied upon for daily survival. The urge remains, however, woven into our DNA. Enter the athlete, who becomes a lightning rod for the release of these instincts. "The main function of sport today lies in the cathartic discharge of the aggressive urge," Lorenz wrote. "It educates man to a conscious and responsible control of his own fighting behavior." This refers to spectators as well as participants. "The most important function of sport lies in furnishing a healthy safety valve for the most indispensable and, at the same time, most dangerous form of aggression."

We do not watch football only for the tight spiral or open

field run, but also for the bone-crushing hit that causes a ball carrier's helmet to fly off and sends trainers rushing onto the field. We do not watch boxing primarily because of the balletic movements of the competitors. We watch it for the knockout punch, the moment when a fist collides with a face with such violence that the victim collapses to the canvas. As Joyce Carol Oates wrote in her incisive *On Boxing*, "spectators at boxing matches relive the murderous infancy of the race." Of course this is not new. It is just that increasingly sophisticated media has amplified the carnage, brought it closer, made it louder and more graphic. Violence is now packaged and sanitized for efficient delivery to the spectator, safe in his chair, whether that be at home or in the arena. During these moments of concentrated ritual mayhem, we can play out our own violent fantasies, we can discharge the pent-up frustrations of a long workweek or a demanding home life, without involving lawyers or the police. Conn Smythe, the father of Canadian hockey, supposedly once quipped that if they did not do something about all the fighting in the game, then they would have to print more tickets. He was a man who understood something essential about both the athlete and the people who came to watch him.

This aggression does not need to involve outright violence to serve its cathartic role. John McEnroe's famous temper tantrums on the genteel lawns of Wimbledon may have left tennis traditionalists red-faced with spluttering outrage, but it also turned him into a cult hero among a generation of young British fans who found in his rage an echo of their own anger and impatience at their society's stultifying traditions. Even spectators who voiced disapproval continued to watch avidly. It is unlikely many people boycotted tennis tournaments in the early 1980s because they were concerned about McEnroe's behavior.

Whether or not this process is as effectively cathartic as Lorenz hoped is a matter of debate. Certainly it is remarkable that tens of thousands of people can gather to watch an intensely violent football game or boxing match, then file out of the stadium in an orderly manner, overseen by a handful of police and stewards. On the other hand, one would be hard-pressed to tell relatives of the Juventus soccer fans who were crushed to death in 1985 while fleeing rioting Liverpool supporters, or the dozens of blacks lynched after Jack Johnson defended his heavyweight crown, that violence has been purged by the contest. If anything, it has been stoked. And it is not just among fans that aggression finds inadequate outlets. Team hazing rituals, especially among younger players, can take a vicious turn, as seen in 2003, when older members of a Long Island high school football squad were accused of sodomizing underclassmen with broomsticks and pinecones during a training camp.

The brutalizing effect of athlete-worship does not only emerge in terrifying outbursts of physical violence. It can also be seen in the way competition, aggression, and a win-at-all-costs mentality seeps into daily interactions in business, politics, and even personal relationships. Terms like *victory lap*, *slam dunk*, and *blindsided* have become commonplace in our discourse, and not necessarily because the user believes that sports lend ennobling values like fair play and camaraderie to our daily lives. Corporate employees are taught that they need to be part of the team, and that there is always another team that needs to be crushed. Teddy Roosevelt believed that the athlete was the greatest exemplar of his nation's core values. In our time of predatory lending, leveraged buyouts, political gamesmanship, and television reality shows that pit contestants in ruthless competition, he just may be right.

The acting out of spectator aggression has had particular significance for black athletes in the United States. An important part of the "black style" that developed during the long era of segregation was a reliance on taunts and trash-talking. Although white ears initially heard these insults as the immediate precursors to murderous violence, blacks understood that it was usually nothing more than a version of the gamesmanship that had been going on since Achilles' Greeks taunted one another outside the walls of Troy. The trash-talking player was simply trying to get inside his opponent's head, to distract him from the task at hand by speaking ill of his mother or reminding him of past defeats.

Once black athletes began to play in formerly white professional leagues, this practice became an important aspect of their game. End zone dances and post-dunk posturing developed into part of the black athlete's lexicon of gamesmanship; his dress and music were seen to derive from urban neighborhoods gripped by drugs and gang violence. While black players and spectators could see these displays as just being part of the game, an expression of the athlete's power and freedom, the white establishment was often shocked. The baggy shorts and swagger of the Fab Five black freshmen of the University of Michigan in 1991, for example, elicited howls of outrage from white alumni. That same year, the brash style of the largely black national champion University of Miami football team was deemed so offensive by the NCAA that it changed its rule book to outlaw the team's more outrageous displays, such as miming gunfire directed at opponents. In 2005, NBA commissioner David Stern instituted a mandatory dress code for league players that explicitly banned them from wearing apparel such as Timberland boots and "do-rags," which were associated with gangs and the hip-hop lifestyle. Administrators and conservative commentators might have wagged their fingers, but these black athletes developed a powerful following among a growing segment of fans, many of them young whites who were also buying hip-hop albums in the millions. Even though the athlete had become less likely to provide a role model for how to be good, he could still be relied on to put on a riveting demonstration of how to be bad.

As spectators come to know the "humanized" athlete better and discover that they do not really like him, there is a growing tendency to dehumanize him in order to maintain his purity. Faced with free agency, astronomical salaries, performance-enhancing drugs, and off-the-field scandals, a growing segment of fans take comfort in thinking of the athlete as a jumble of numbers, nothing more than the sum total of his performances. The last few decades have seen the rise of this statistical athlete. Of course, the practice of measuring performances has been going on for centuries, starting in earnest with the invention of the stopwatch in the early 19th century. Perhaps the most important early moment in the development of the athlete's mathematical identity was Henry Chadwick's creation of the box score in 1859. Ruth's 714 career home runs, Maris's 61 in a single season, DiMaggio's barely comprehensible 56-game hitting streak; Triple Crowns, Grand Slams, test centuries—athletes were known by numbers they etched in the public's imagination. In ancient Greece, the only way two competitors could be compared was if they met face-to-face. Now, men who meet only a few times each season are cast in fierce competition for the same batting title.

There was always a sense, however, that mere numbers were not the measure of the man. Athletes were deemed to be more than just their records. What is the statistical value of Willie Mays's over-the-shoulder catch of Vic Wertz's smash in the first game of the 1954 World Series? On paper, it is one out, though anyone who understands the first thing about baseball knows it is much more than that. How do you tally a goal scored by a Pelé bicycle kick or a Beckham set piece? Surely not with the same value you would give to a header scored by a team down 4 to 0 in "garbage time" at the end of a game. Statistics can only ever tell us so much. Sometimes they can tell us nothing at all.

Recently, a growing group of fans have challenged this view. They believe that, if only applied with sufficient rigor, numbers *can* tell us everything. The sort of statistical analysis that think tanks like the RAND Corporation once brought to bear on multinational corporations or the conduct of war is now used with often mind-boggling elaboration to rate athletic performance. The Bowl Championship Series (BCS) rankings that determine which two teams compete for the NCAA football crown comprise a byzantine mix of traditional polls and six computer ranking systems, whose formulas are secret but are said to include variables such as wins, losses, game location, and strength of schedule. Tennis and golf ranking systems are also growing increasingly complex. A number one ranking is no longer the opinion of a bunch of sportswriters or coaches. It is put forward as being as cold and hard a fact as the temperature outside.

The most advanced attempt to create an arithmetical identity for the athlete comes from baseball writer and statistician Bill James. Starting in the late 1970s, James began publishing increasingly complex analyses of baseball statistics in order to evaluate past as well as predict future performances. His approach is part of the broader "sabermetrics" movement (after the Society for American Baseball Research), which views mathematics as the key to unlocking the mysteries of the game. In James's case, number crunching can determine such new categories as "runs created" and "Pythagorean winning percentage." It also comes up with "similarity scores" that allow players of different generations to be compared with one another to determine which stars of the past best resemble those of the present day. Comparable algorithms exist for basketball and football. Entering this "sabermetrical" world is more akin to stepping inside a sealed room containing a humming super computer than a ballpark on a sultry summer afternoon.

Fantasy leagues are another increasingly popular symptom of the trend toward reducing athletes to statistics. Created in the 1960s as an elaborate board game for baseball enthusiasts, computerized fantasy leagues that involve sophisticated software are now available for sports ranging from football to NASCAR. Statistics generated on actual fields of play might be essential for determining winners and losers in these leagues, but equally important are the decisions of the fantasy owner when compiling his team. In an era of callous stars and franchises that are liable to fragment at the end of even a championship season, this gives the alienated fan the ability to exercise control over the athlete by serving as both his manager and owner. The fact that it is all make-believe does not stop tens of millions from participating.

Nor does it prevent an equally vast number of fans, most of them boys and young men, from spending long hours playing video games like *Madden NFL*. Here the control over the athlete is even more direct. The fan's ability to manipulate avatars provides a virtual intimacy that player strikes, trades, tantrums, and felony arrests make awkward in daily life. In many of these games, a player can even give his own name to a custom-built athlete. The ability to identify with the competitor, always a central part of his appeal, comes close to being absolute.

The dehumanization of the athlete is not only taking place in the digital and numeric worlds. Technology is also threatening to transform the competitor himself into something not-quite-human. Performance-enhancing drugs, surgery, prosthetics, even sports psychology are altering athletes in ways hard work and a good diet could have never achieved. Despite strenuous efforts on the part of sports governors, the athlete of the future may be an entirely different beast than his predecessors.

The most obvious transformation of the athlete's body is one that has been taking place since at least the 1970s, when the East German government decided to treat its athletes like factory chickens in order to establish the supremacy of their socialist system. Not that the West was any better. In the United States and Europe, however, the free market allowed individual competitors the liberty to pump their bodies full of steroids without government interference. Their actions may not have been ethical, but they were understandable, given the fate of Western athletes who had been stampeded by beefed-up Eastern Bloc rivals in the 1970s. Consider the case of the American swimmer Shirley Babashoff, who should by rights be remembered as one of the greatest competitors in her sport's history. Going into the 1976 Olympics, she was considered a favorite to win multiple individual gold medals, only to lose three times to East German swimmers. When subsequent American athletes discovered that Babashoff was making ends meet as a letter carrier in her post-Olympic career, the temptation to dope must have become very powerful.

By the 1980s, performance-enhancing drugs were widespread throughout the sports world. Not all athletes were dirty, but nearly all of them suspected that some of their competitors were. Although the IOC had started drug testing athletes in 1968, the first big headline case came in the 1988 Seoul Games, when, immediately after winning the 100-meter dash in world-record time, the Canadian sprinter Ben Johnson tested positive for stanozolol, a steroid used to fatten cattle. Johnson's muscle-knotted physique and yellowish eyes presented an image of the athlete that was monstrously new. The fact that this formerly competent sprinter had been transformed into an unbeatable running machine simply by sticking a hypodermic needle in his arm subverted centuries of inherited wisdom about vigorous practice and innate talent.

The next two decades saw crisis after crisis arise around the issue of performance-enhancing drugs. Although a series of high-profile track and field athletes continued to test positive, attention switched to the baseball diamond, where home runs, one of the purest emanations of muscle power in all of sports, were becoming increasingly common. The 1998 duel between Mark McGwire and Sammy Sosa to break the single–season home run mark felt as if it was ushering in a new era. Maybe it was, since both men were subsequently shown to have used steroids, Sosa in a 2003 test, McGwire in a 2010 confession. Cheating had come a long way from the wad of spit or dollop of Vaseline players had once used to doctor the ball. As Barry Bonds began to tear up the records books in the early years of the 21st century, a jaded public was hardly surprised when accusations began to swirl that he had used an anabolic steroid called "The Clear." To many, the absence of definitive proof did not mean that he was innocent. It simply showed that he was too clever to get caught.

Not all science, however, was tainted with the stink of the illicit. Some athletes used technology as a way of overcoming obstacles that would have kept them from competing just a few years earlier. Even so, these good faith efforts were not without some deeply troubling dimensions. Take the case of the South African sprinter Oscar Pistorius. Born without fibula bones, Pistorius had both legs amputated below the knee while he was still an infant. Undaunted, he began to compete in track and field with the help of prosthetics, eventually employing a cutting-edge device known as the Cheetah Flex-Foot carbon fiber transtibial artificial limb. Using this J-shaped apparatus, Pistorius became the world's top Paralympic sprinter. It was when he started to run in meets for able-bodied competitors in 2007, turning in times that put him on the cusp of being among the top sprinters in the world, that the controversy began. After protests, the IAAF passed a rule that banned "any technical device that incorporates springs, wheels or any other element that provides a user with an advantage over another athlete not using such a device." Although

Pistorius was initially prohibited from trying out for the 2008 Beijing Olympics, an appeals panel overturned the ban, saying that the IAAF had not presented sufficient evidence to prove that the Cheetah gave Pistorius a competitive edge. In the end, it was only his performances just outside the qualifying standards that kept him from being the first amputee runner to compete in the Olympics. Pistorius's case shows that, as with performance-enhancing drugs, we are entering an era when rules will always be one step behind science. The Age of the Asterisk may soon be upon us, when all performances will be subject to disclaimers and doubt.

For now, however, the athlete continues to hold his own. Despite all the efforts to commodify and dehumanize him, he retains the ability to make spectators suspend disbelief as they watch him compete. Not even the athlete's own excesses have been able to irreparably shatter the icon. McEnroe's behavior during his 1980 Wimbledon semifinal against Jimmy Connors may have caused the normally reserved Centre Court crowd to jeer as he entered for the final against Björn Borg, but by the end of their riveting fourth-set tiebreaker, the greatest 20 minutes of tennis ever played, all had been forgiven. People understood that they were watching something special. The spell had been cast. The run-up to the 2011 college football national championship was rife with rumors that Auburn's Heisman Trophy–winning quarterback Cam Newton had sold his services to the highest bidder when choosing a college. As Newton led his team to a thrilling victory, however, many of those who had been bad-mouthing him just hours earlier were now proclaiming him a hero.

Perhaps the day is coming when performance-enhancing

drugs and fantasy technology will turn the athlete into a robot or a cluster of pixels, but we are not yet there. We are not ready to grant him the "total difference in power" Pindar wrote about in his ode, to remove him from the realm of the human by making him a monster or a god. For us to identify with the athlete, to thrill in his performances, he still needs to be like us. We still need a vital connection to him. Even if he fails us as a political icon or "role model," we still require his most intense and sublime moments of competition. We need him to stop time, to pull us out of our lives for the duration of a thrilling play or game or race. At his best, the athlete takes us to a place where the rules are clear, where defeat can always be redeemed by victory, and where the end of a season only means that a new one will soon begin.

This shamanistic power was starkly apparent on July 19, 1996, when Muhammad Ali made a surprise appearance to light the Olympic flame at the opening ceremony of the Atlanta Games. It was, at first, a shocking sight. The effects of his Parkinson's disease were painfully evident. His stiff, mincing walk gave a whole new meaning to the term "Ali Shuffle." That once-lively face was now a bewildered mask. The left arm that had punished opponents with deadly accurate jabs shook uncontrollably. In order to make things easier for Ali, event organizers had rigged a cable to carry the flame from his platform to the massive torch atop the stadium. Even this proved difficult for this once supremely agile man—Ali burned himself while lighting the flammable patch of the cable. The ceremony reached its preordained climax; both the torch and the crowd erupted. The television announcer explained to the millions of viewers that they were witnessing "a poignant figure."

As if anyone needed to be told. It is difficult to imagine a more diminished character than the frail, quivering athlete who emerged from the shadows at the Centennial Olympic Stadium on that summer night. It was Lear on his blasted heath, only this time his decline was being broadcast live to hundreds of millions of viewers. Whoever had decided to put Ali up there understood the image's haunting power. He seemed more than just weak. He had been silenced, this man who had twenty five years earlier told Norman Mailer, "I'd die if I couldn't talk." Where spectators had once perched on the edge of their seats to find out if Ali-the-champion could prevail against some of the most fearsome heavyweights of all time, now the suspense came from seeing if Ali-the-invalid could execute the most rudimentary of acts.

And yet we cheered. We gave him our reverence. Undoubtedly, some of this was in response to the moment's stage-managed pathos. Years of programming had trained us to react as expected to the image of the sick athlete. But there was something deeper at work than just good television. Through some powerful alchemy, the image of the fading man conjured the eternal in him. Many of us had grown up with Ali. His victories and defeats made up a calendar that marked the stages of our lives. The producers and the advertisers presented us with a trembling figure in an ill-fitting T-shirt as a way to boost ratings and further enhance their five-ringed brand. But we saw beyond that. We saw the exhausted warrior in Manila who somehow withstood the withering attacks of a relentless Joe Frazier to win a fight that is still judged by many to be the most punishing in modern championship history. A fight that Ali would afterward describe as the "closest thing to dying that I know of." They wanted us to pity him, but we chose to recall the man as he came off the ropes to defeat a seemingly invincible

George Foreman in Zaire in a contest some veteran observers thought Ali might not even survive. We remembered the young boxer, who stood over Sonny Liston after hitting him with a punch so sudden that few even saw it. And then went home to write poetry about it. Finally, we saw a very different Olympian from this sad, brittle figure. We saw the lean, handsome 18-year-old kid with the Roman senator's name who stood on a podium in the Italian capital's Palazzo dello Sport thirty six years earlier, not far from where the *munera* were once held, to accept a gold medal that legend claims he would later throw into the Ohio River to protest his nation's racism. Back then, the future seemed to belong to him. In Atlanta, it still did. Olympian, gladiator, rebel, religious warrior, freedom fighter, Ali would forever remind us of the eternal possibilities of the athlete.

SELECTED BIBLIOGRAPHY

Auguet, Roland. *Cruelty and Civilization: The Roman Games*. London: Routledge, 1994.

Barker, Juliet R. V. *The Tournament in England 1100–1400*. Woodbridge, England: Boydell Press, 2003.

Boddy, Kasia. *Boxing: A Cultural History*. London: Reaktion Books, 2008.

Creamer, Robert W. *Babe: The Legend Comes to Life*. New York: Simon & Schuster, 1974.

de Troyes, Chretien. *Cliges: A Romance*. Translated by L. J. Gardiner. New York: Cooper Square Publishers, 1966.

Egan, Pierce. *Boxiana; or, Sketches of Ancient and Modern Pugilism*. Chestnut Hill: Adamant Media Corporation, 2001.

Exley, Frederick. *A Fan's Notes*. New York: Vintage, 1988.

Fitzgerald, F. Scott. *The Great Gatsby*. New York: Scribner, 1925.

Futrell, Alison. *Blood in the Arena: The Spectacle of Roman Power*. Austin: University of Texas, 1997.

Galeano, Eduardo. *Soccer in Sun and Shadow*. Translated by Mark Fried. London: Verso, 2003.

Guttmann, Allen. *Sports: The First Five Millennia*. Amherst: University of Massachusetts Press, 2004.

Halberstam, David. *Playing for Keeps: Michael Jordan and the World He Made*. New York: Three Rivers Press, 2000.

Holt, Richard. *Sport and the British: A Modern History*. Oxford University Press, 1989.

Homer. *The Iliad*. Translated by Robert Fagles. New York: Viking. 1990.

Huizinga, Johan. *Homo Ludens: A Study of the Play-Element in Culture*. Boston: Beacon Press, 1971.

Lorenz, Konrad. *On Aggression*. Translated by Marjorie Kerr Wilson. New York: Harcourt, Brace & World, 1966.

Mandell, Richard A. *Sport: A Cultural History*. New York: Columbia University Press, 1984.

Mangan, J. A. *Athleticism in the Victorian and Edwardian Public School*. Cambridge University Press, 1981.

Miller, Stephen G. *Ancient Greek Athletics.* New Haven: Yale University Press, 2006.

Oates, Joyce Carol. *On Boxing.* New York: Harper Perennial, 2006.

Rhoden, William C. *Forty Million Dollar Slaves: The Rise, Fall, and Redemption of the Black Athlete.* New York: Crown, 2006.

Scott, Jack. *The Athletic Revolution.* New York: McMillan, 1982.

Suetonius. *The Twelve Caesars.* Translated by Robert Graves. New York: Penguin Classic, 2007.

Wallechinsky, David, and Jaime Loucky. *The Complete Book of the Olympics.* London: Aurum Press. 2008.

Young, David C. *The Olympic Myth of Greek Amateur Athletics.* Chicago: Ares Publishers, 1984.

INDEX